THE

EUROPEAN UNION

EXPLAINED

THE
EUROPEAN
UNION
EXPLAINED

Andreas Staab

Institutions · Actors · Global Impact

Indiana University Press
Bloomington · Indianapolis

This book is a publication of

Indiana University Press
601 North Morton Street
Bloomington, IN 47404-3797 USA

http://iupress.indiana.edu

Telephone orders	800-842-6796
Fax orders	812-855-7931
Orders by e-mail	iuporder@indiana.edu

The paper used in this publication meets the minimum requirements of American National Standard for Information Sciences—Permanence of Paper for
Printed Library Materials, ANSI Z39.48-1984.

Manufactured in the United States of America

Library of Congress Cataloging-in-Publication Data

Staab, Andreas, date-
  The European Union explained : institutions, actors, global impact / Andreas
Staab.
     p. cm.
  Includes bibliographical references and index.
  ISBN 978-0-253-35233-0 (cloth) — ISBN 978-0-253-22018-9 (pbk.) 1. Euro-
pean Union. I. Title.
  JN30.S713 2008
  341.242'2—dc22

                                                            2008013131

1 2 3 4 5 13 12 11 10 09 08

To Sophia and Luisa.
Europeans by birth and maybe even by choice.

Contents

Preface

The European Union (EU) today differs considerably from the integration project that began in the 1950s. Initially conceived as a way to safeguard peace and enable economic recovery among six Western European countries, the EU has developed into one of the world's most formidable trading blocs spanning much of the European continent. Its future, however, is very much in flux. The recent controversies over the ratification of a constitutional treaty and disagreements concerning policy reforms and how to finance them has once again evoked fundamental disagreements over the future direction of the EU. Given the prospect of still more countries lining up to join, some member states argue against further political integration whereas others continue to push for ambitious policy and institutional reforms.

Regardless of the outcome of this debate, the European Union represents a hugely influential vehicle for organizing Europe and constitutes a unique experiment of "deep" international cooperation. Economically it has boosted prosperity levels. Politically it has fostered the democratic transition of former fascist and communist dictatorships, and has also helped to overcome the artificial division of Europe caused by the Iron Curtain and the Cold War. On the other hand, the EU has often been criticized for favoring big business over the economic, social, and political needs of its citizens. Others accuse the EU of lacking transparency and accountability in its institutional processes, and some claim that European integration has led to the gradual erosion of national and cultural differences and traditions.

For these reasons the EU remains a highly intriguing subject, as it offers clear examples of the impact of politics on societies. The EU is not the European equivalent of the United States of America, but it is also much more than a traditional international organization. Throughout its existence, European leaders have continually been faced with far-reaching decisions: Which issues are better organized at the EU level and which should remain under the domain of the nation-state? Must member states give up parts of their national sovereignty for the sake of creating an ever closer union? To what extent should national differences prevail on how to organize a society's political, economic, social, and cultural spheres? From these perspectives, the past decades of the European integration project have given us valuable lessons in state building and the choices confronting political leaders and citizens.

This book offers a broad overview of the politics and policies of the European Union. Part 1 focuses on the key economic and political parameters but also the main actors and processes that have shaped the EU integration process, concluding with a discussion of enlargement that charts the development of the EU into a union of twenty-seven member states. Part 2 discusses the EU's institutional mechanisms and main actors, and part 3 deals with crucial policies and their impact on European societies and the wider world.

In recent years the EU has been the subject of a broad range of books and academic articles. To my knowledge, however, the overwhelming majority of publications are directed at an audience already tuned in to the language of political science and its related analytical and methodological concepts. Postgraduate and academic readership in particular seems to have a comprehensive library of materials on the EU. On the other hand, a number of publications portray the EU in a rather basic and rudimentary light. This book aims to close this gap by offering an in-depth yet concise introduction to the European Union and its institutions and polices in a style accessible to undergraduate as well as high school students, indeed to any reader, young or old, academic or professional, with an interest in politics and history. To provide a coherent understanding of the subject, I highlight a number of key issues surrounding the main areas of debate and controversy. For those seeking more advanced study, a list of publications organized according to the book's chapters is provided at the end.

Acknowledgments

This book first took shape as a series of handouts designed for participants of seminars organized by EPIC—the European Policy Information Centre, which itself originated within the European Institute at the London School of Economics, where I taught until the summer of 2000. During that year a number of colleagues encouraged me to establish EPIC as an independent training agency and consultancy. Over the years we have been fortunate to work with civil servants, ministers, Supreme Court judges, businesspeople, and representatives from the nonprofit sector, as well as high school and university students from a number of EU accession and candidate countries. Thus the book has been shaped by the experiences of those for whom the EU is of practical relevance in their professional lives, as well as of individuals for whom Europe represents a panacea that may ultimately deliver political stability and economic prosperity.

Working with people for whom English is not their mother tongue, our courses, of necessity, were conducted in a style stripped of excessive academic jargon. It was Martin Lodge, a former colleague from the London School of Economics and a current EPIC associate, who suggested that the course handouts that accompany our seminars would be suitable for an undergraduate and indeed a nonacademic audience, and thus this book was born.

Several colleagues and friends of the EPIC family have offered much appreciated guidance and support, enabling me to narrow my own knowledge gaps and enhance my understanding of EU affairs. I am indebted to Eiko Thielemann and Martin Lodge, who added factual and analytical depth to the text. Charles Dannreuther was behind the conceptualization of the first chapter, and Karen Smith, should she ever tire of academia, would make a wonderful copy editor. My thanks also go to John Bedingfield for providing me with greater insight into the working mechanisms of the EU's Cohesion Policy, to Bruce Ross who repeated this trick for the Common Agricultural Policy, and to Bob Hancké who improved my understanding of Economic and Monetary Union.

EPIC would not have survived, nor would this book have been written, without the help of partner organizations that supported us in running our training exercises. I am forever grateful to the British Council and especially Roy Cross, Isabelle van de Gejuchte, Andrew Hadley, Marina Ioannou, Elizabeta Jovanovska, Bob Ness, Peter Skelton, Monica Tantele, and Sencan Yesilada. From the Croatian Ministry of Foreign Affairs and European Integration, Tatjana Corlija and Sandra Trvtkovic deserve a special thank you. From the British Foreign and Commonwealth Office, Jonathan Allen, David Austin, Yilmaz Ahmetoglu, Philip Barton, Ambassador Edward Clay, Matt Field, Richard Jones, Jill Morris, Ambassador Lyn Parker, and Ivana Vukov were great sources of support and encouragement. From the European Commission, Ambassador Donato Chiarini deserves praise for never shying away from a debate about EU affairs, even if it meant that his employer was placed sometimes under uncomfortable scrutiny. Lastly, for constantly testing the accuracy and suitability of this material, I thank my American students, who spent a semester in London as part of their study abroad programs.

Acronyms

ACP	Asia, Caribbean, and Pacific
AFSJ	Area of Freedom, Security, and Justice
CARDS	Community Assistance for Reconstruction, Development, and Stabilization
CAP	Common Agricultural Policy
CCP	Common Commercial Policy
CEPOL	European Police College
CFSP	Common Foreign and Security Policy
CIS	Commonwealth of Independent States
COMECON	Council for Mutual Economic Assistance
COPA	Committee of Professional Agricultural Organization
COREPER	Committee of Permanent Representatives
EBA	Everything But Arms
EC	European Community (merger of EEC, ECSC, and Euratom treaties)
EC	Economic Community (Pillar I of Maastricht Treaty)
ECB	European Central Bank
ECM	European Common Market
ECOFIN	Council of Economic and Finance Ministers
ECSC	European Coal and Steel Community
ECU	European Currency Unit
EDC	European Defense Community
EEA	European Economic Area

EEC	European Economic Community
EFTA	European Free Trade Association
ELO	European Liaison Officer
EMS	European Monetary System
EMU	Economic and Monetary Union
ENP	European Neighborhood Policy
ENPI	European Neighborhood and Partnership Instrument
EP	European Parliament
EPC	European Political Cooperation
ERDF	European Regional Development Fund
ERF	European Refuge Fund
ERP	European Recovery Program
ESF	European Social Fund
EU	European Union
EURATOM	European Atomic Energy Community
EUROJUST	European Judicial Unit
EUROPOL	European Police Office
ESCB	European System of Central Banks
ESDP	European Security and Defense Policy
FRONTEX	European Agency for the Management of Operational Cooperation at the External Borders
GAERC	General Affairs and External Relations Council
GATS	General Agreement on Trade in Services
GATT	General Agreement on Tariffs and Trade
GCC	Gulf Cooperation Council
GDP	Gross Domestic Product
ICTY	International Criminal Tribunal for the Former Yugoslavia
IGC	Intergovernmental Conference
ISPA	Instrument for Structural Policies for Pre-Accession
JHA	Justice and Home Affairs
MARRI	Migration, Asylum, Refugees Regional Initiative
MEP	Member of the European Parliament
NATO	North Atlantic Treaty Organization
NRC	NATO Russian Council
OCA	Optimum Currency Area
OECD	Organization for Economic Cooperation and Development
OEEC	Organization for European Economic Cooperation
OPEC	Organization of the Petroleum Exporting Countries
PHARE	Poland/Hungary Assistance for Reconstruction of Economies
SAA	Stabilization and Association Agreement
SAP	Stabilization and Association Process

SAPARD	Special Program of Pre-Accession for Agriculture and Rural Development
QMV	Qualified Majority Voting
SEA	Single European Act
SEM	Single European Market
SPUC	Society for the Protection of Unborn Children
TAIEX	Technical Assistance Information Exchange Instrument
TEU	Treaty on the European Union
TRIM	Trade Related Investment Issues
TRIPS	General Agreement on Intellectual Property Rights
TRNC	Turkish Republic of Northern Cyprus
UNMIK	United Nations Mission in Kosovo
VAT	Value Added Tax
VER	Voluntary Export Restraints
WEU	Western European Union
WTO	World Trade Organization

Tables

PART ONE

THE EVOLUTION OF THE
EUROPEAN UNION

1

Parameters of European Integration

Given the multitude of treaties, political actors, and policies, trying to gain an understanding of European integration can indeed be a daunting task. Coming to terms with the European Union is further complicated by often confusing official terminology with similar sounding names. What is the difference, after all, between the European Council, the Council of Europe, and the Council of the European Union? And exactly how does the European Community differ from the European Economic Community and the European Union? In answering these questions, this chapter introduces the key processes, actors, and developments that have shaped European integration ever since the start of the project in the 1950s. The key issues are the following:

1. The factors contributing to early European cooperation that were common to all West European states or relevant only in certain countries.
2. Policies, political actors, and political developments involved in supranational or intergovernmental integration.
3. The Eurosclerosis of the 1970s that resulted from the Luxembourg Compromise in the 1960s.
4. The re-launch of European integration in the 1980s.

5. The 2001 Treaty of Nice and its goal of preparing the European Union for enlargement to Central and Eastern Europe.
6. The impact in 2007 of the proposed Reform Treaty on the future development of the European Union.

The Concept of European Integration

European integration is most frequently associated with the period after the end of the Second World War, as Western European states increasingly cooperated during various developmental stages of the European Union. But the concept of governing Europe actually has a far longer history. From the Roman Empire of Julius Caesar, to Napoleon, Hitler, and Stalin, European history is marked by many attempts to organize the multitude of nations and ethnicities into a more or less coherent political entity with competing views of how the different states should be related and the degree to which autonomy and sovereignty should be preserved. Nonetheless, though the concept of an integrated Europe is not new, without question the European Union, the most recent vehicle for organizing Europe, has, to date, been a highly successful attempt at integration.

Minimalism vs. Maximalism

With the end of the Second World War, debates over European integration again dominated the political agenda. Europe had just been through one of the most damaging and catastrophic events mankind had ever experienced, and there was a pressing need for an organizational vehicle that finally would be able to deliver peace and ultimately prosperity. The debates centered on two different views of European integration that would characterize many of the future discussions on the subject. The "maximalist" view called for a federal structure with the goal of establishing the United States of Europe, whereas the "minimalist" view envisioned a loose union based largely on trade relations between sovereign member states. The maximalists were personified by the Italian political philosopher Altiero Spinelli, and the minimalists were championed by the former prime minister of the United Kingdom Winston Churchill. Churchill's position developed from the perspective of a European country that did not endure fascist occupation and that emerged victorious from World War II. The UK could also look back on a strong democratic tradition, a powerful Commonwealth, and strong political and economic links with the United States. Borrowing heavily from the German philosopher Immanuel Kant and his work on "Perpetual Peace," Churchill, in a famous speech in Zurich in 1946, argued that one way of establishing peace would be to forge closer ties among the peoples of Europe through stronger trade relations. The prospect of war would then be greatly reduced, since any possible hostilities across borders would threaten one's potential customers. Churchill, confusingly, termed this project the "United States

Table 1.1. Minimalism vs. Maximalism

Minimalism	Maximalism
• Winston Churchill	• Altiero Spinelli
• Safeguard peace through an economic union (Kant: trading nations do not go to war with one another)	• Economic ties alone are not enough to prevent conflict between nations
• Economic union only	• Economic and political union

of Europe," but in reality it was a watered-down version of what America's Founding Fathers had in mind.

Establishing peace along the lines of a trading union did not go far enough for Spinelli. After all, a loose economic union could not be expected to keep in check the rise of another dictator such as Hitler or Stalin. Hence Spinelli argued that only the combination of an economic and a political union could secure long-term peaceful conditions; he had even written a draft constitution for a federal Europe while imprisoned by Mussolini during the Second World War. Spinelli's supporters had often been accused of envisioning the end of the nation-state in Europe. But, in fact, Spinelli's view, which grew from the resistance movement in Nazi-occupied Europe where fascism had gravely undermined the nation-state, actually embraced European integration as essential to rescuing the nation-state after two devastating world wars and periods of economic and political instability.

Despite differences in their political objectives, both maximalism and mini-malism—both Spinelli and Churchill—supported greater links between European nations. With Europeans assessing the scale of devastation, support for European integration in the aftermath of World War II propelled the European Union (EU) into existence. However, the precise modalities of how the Union should be organized and, in particular, the degree of national sovereignty that should be surrendered for the sake of closer integration remains to this date the essence of the European integration.

Intergovernmentalism versus Supranationalism

At the beginning of the postwar European project, two concepts emerged about how integration could be implemented: supranationalism and intergovernmentalism. With supranationalism, institutions and policies supersede the power of their national equivalents. The European Court of Justice, for example, could issue verdicts that nullify and supersede verdicts reached by national courts. Similarly, supranational policies are implemented as political programs that replace their national equivalents. An example is Economic and Monetary Union (EMU), where the EU's single currency, the Euro, replaces national currencies.

Table 1.2. Concepts of European Integration

Intergovernmentalism	Supranationalism
• Integration through cooperation between national governments; no new institutions	• Integration by establishing new institutions and policies that rise above the national sovereignty of member states
• Example: EU foreign policy	• Example: Single European currency

Intergovernmentalism, in contrast, minimizes the creation of new institutions and policies, and conducts European integration through cooperation between national governments. This approach is illustrated in the realm of foreign policy. The EU does not have a foreign minister or a secretary of state, as there is no EU foreign policy worth speaking of, unless all the member state governments agree on an issue. In the case of the war in Iraq, the EU split into two camps, one supporting George Bush's military intervention and the other supporting continued inspections by the envoy of the United Nations Hans Blix. In light of these two opposing viewpoints a compromise simply could not be reached, which meant that the EU did not have a common foreign policy regarding Iraq. On the other hand, all member states condemned apartheid in South Africa in the late 1980s, and the EU as a whole imposed economic sanctions on that country.

The Impact of the Second World War

In the aftermath of World War II, all European states had the staggering problem of reconstructing their economies, and Europe needed, above all, peace and stability. The war had left 5.5 million soldiers and 9.5 million civilians dead. In Germany and Great Britain alone, 7 million homes were damaged or destroyed; across Europe, 50 million people were homeless, and cities and towns were in ruins. Europe was facing mountainous challenges. The objective of any responsible government, therefore, was quite obvious: to establish relatively peaceful conditions that would enable the rebuilding of economies, and here, in particular, a largely destroyed infrastructure. The threat of famine was a real-life possibility. Rail networks and roads needed to be replaced, water, heating, and electricity restored, and houses rebuilt—all in the face of the additional problem of millions of refugees fleeing to the West from the advancing communist empire in Central and Eastern Europe. Against these monumental challenges, the first priority was to limit the possibility of a renewed conflict. A potential reemergence of hostilities, the advent of a new antagonistic regime, of military conflict, whether on the scale of a civil war or across borders, would have been catastrophic. But what to do?

The Treaty of Versailles in the aftermath of World War I had presented Europe with a bitter lesson: punishing the aggressors (Germany and Austria) with stifling reparation payments had contributed to the gradual implosion of the Weimar Republic and the eventual rise of fascism, which plunged the continent into another major crisis, only twenty years after the previous one presumably had been resolved. Perhaps a new approach of conciliation and integration would serve Europe better.

In this environment, it seemed necessary for the United States to motivate the continent into action. To do so, the U.S. supplied more than $13 billion through the European Recovery Program (ERP), more commonly known as the Marshall Plan. This generous support is explained largely as an effort to block the spread of Soviet Communism to Western Europe. First and foremost, key policy makers in the U.S. feared a shift in political orientation in Europe toward the East and the Soviet Union and away from the United States. Many postwar national elections reflected a mood for change, favoring left-oriented parties that had gained significant support in France, Italy, Greece, and the United Kingdom. In addition, West European states appeared unable to provide food and other basic necessities in the period immediately after the war. The U.S. feared that this crisis could easily erupt into political instability, with communist and potentially even resurgent fascist movements able to gain the political support of a disillusioned electorate. The goal of Marshall Aid, therefore, aimed to cement the introduction of market-oriented and capitalist economic systems, which ultimately would establish links across the Atlantic and away from the Soviet Union. Finally, America's isolationist policies of the 1930s simply had not worked, as democratic European states, left to their own devices, were unable to contain the expansionist drive of fascism. Thus the Truman administration adopted a more proactive strategy in its foreign policy objectives.

American support provided a compelling financial incentive for cooperation that had not existed before. The result was the Organization for European Economic Cooperation (OEEC), subsequently renamed the Organization of Economic Cooperation and Development (OECD), which essentially was set up by the U.S. to ensure that the Marshall Plan money was distributed in an organized fashion. The OEEC also provided a framework in which European states were introduced to economic cooperation in an institutionalized setting and across national borders. The OEEC, then, was the forum where West European states prepared for the first attempts at supranational integration.

In 1949, shortly after the establishment of the OEEC, the European states created the Council of Europe, which evolved from a Congress held in the Dutch capital of The Hague the previous year and provided a framework of principles for the protection of human rights and key freedoms considered essential to a free and peaceful Europe. The Council of Europe has since become less influential, but it still plays a role through the institutional machinery that it established in the European Court of Human Rights.[1] In the 1940s, however, the Council of Europe was important in promoting the concept of an integrated Europe, although one based on intergovernmentalism and on the autonomy of the nation-state.

The European Coal and Steel Community

The first impetus to supranational integration came mainly from France, especially from one man, Jean Monnet, a senior civil servant with a keen eye for political opportunity.[2] He had learned the advantages of economic planning in the U.S., and he applied the lessons with considerable success in the French planning system that he established after the war. Monnet had a straightforward and, because of its simplicity, ultimately brilliant idea. He envisioned that a supra-nationally regulated Europe-wide market in coal and steel was central to achieving sustained peace in Europe. The brilliance of this idea was that both commodities are essential for war: steel for the production of weapons and coal to provide energy for factories that could produce weapons. Monnet argued that an authority that was independent of national interests could greatly reduce the likelihood of war, at least war on the scale of the previous two world wars. He presented his concept to the French foreign minister Robert Schuman, whose plan (later called the Schuman plan) specified exactly how a European Coal and Steel Community (ECSC) could be created and managed by a "Higher Authority" with "supranational powers." The Schuman plan was not altogether altruistic, for it served the French national interest. Monnet's idea was conceived on the assumption that France would have access to the steel factories and coal reserves of the German Ruhr valley. In the end though, France had to forsake this territorial aspiration as the Ruhr area was kept under German control. However, the incorporation of West Germany into the Marshall Plan meant that the French economy would grow in competition with West German industry rather than on the back of it. As a minor token to the French, the ECSC would at least secure French access to the resources of the Ruhr. At this historical juncture, however, the UK decided not to participate in the budding European project. The reason was, quite simply, that in 1945 the UK had elected a left-leaning Labour Party government that embarked on an ambitious economic program that included nationalization of the coal and steel sector. British Prime Minister Clement Atlee justifiably concluded that it would be impossible to supranationalize an industrial sector that only shortly before was subject to nationalization. This mundane historical development accounted for why the British did not jump on the European bandwagon. As it turned out later, the UK's rejection of the Schuman Plan set the tone for Britain's European policy ever since. Other European countries, however, responded enthusiastically to Monnet's vision; not only France and West Germany but also Italy, the Netherlands, Belgium, and Luxembourg signed up to the ECSC, thereby forming the nucleus of the "original six" that would eventually become the European Union of today.

The ECSC was an important victory for Monnet, as it secured the principle of a supranational form of political organization. The Treaty of Paris in 1951, establishing the ECSC, set up the organizational blueprint for the future. The supranational High Authority was a small body, and thus it depended on the institutions of the member states. Also, on the insistence of Belgium, Luxembourg, and the Netherlands, an

Table 1.3. Summary of EU Treaties

Treaty	Signed	Entered into Force
European Coal and Steel Community	1951	1952
European Economic Community	1957	1958
European Atomic Energy Community	1957	1958
Single European Act	1986	1987
Treaty on the European Union (Maastricht Treaty)	1992	1993
Treaty of Amsterdam	1997	1999
Treaty of Nice	2001	2003
Reform Treaty (Lisbon Treaty)	2007	2009

intergovernmental Council of Ministers was established to safeguard national interests, especially of smaller states. A supranational Court of Justice would enforce the law, and the citizens of Europe were very loosely involved through a supranational Assembly of National Representatives.

Toward a European Defense Community (EDC)

The Korean War from 1950 to 1953 broadened the scope of European integration beyond the simple coal and steel union. The war was widely perceived as a potential precursor to World War III, prompting the U.S. to request military assistance from Europe, arguing, in particular, that a coherent defense of democracy in Europe and the rest of the world would be well advised to take advantage of West Germany's industrial strength. President Truman declared that Germany's military capacities ought to be reintegrated into a wider regional setting. At first France balked at Truman's idea, given the fresh memories of the fatal consequences of Hitler's military might and the prospect of German rearmament. But a new plan emerged, again developed by Monnet, but this time presented by French Prime Minister Pleven; the plan would allow the remilitarization of Germany but only within the organizational setup of a European Defense Community (EDC), which would be controlled by a supranational authority in a way similar to the integration of West German reindustrialization under the ECSC. Even more, discussions between the states concerning the EDC also led to a proposal for a European Political Community, under which related issues of foreign policy could also be decided. At this stage it seemed that a supranational United States of Europe, with a unified military umbrella and a unified foreign policy, was indeed likely.

But the proposals had stretched the idea of European integration to its limit. Although the six negotiating states of the ECSC signed the Treaty on the EDC in 1952, the final proposal failed to be ratified by the French parliament. Thus, much of the impetus for the European Political Community evaporated. Defense cooperation between states was later developed under the weaker Western European Union (WEU),[3] which essentially only provided a consultative forum for the founding members of the ECSC and the UK. The incorporation of such nationally sensitive political areas as foreign policy and defense into a supranational European organizational structure was too ambitious a leap to federalism at such an early stage. In the end, after the integration of West German forces into the North Atlantic Treaty Organization (NATO) in 1955, the idea of a European security umbrella had finally lost momentum.

Toward an Economic Community

Monnet resigned in 1954, primarily so that he could maintain the impetus for European integration at a distance from the exposure that the failure of the EDC had thrust upon him. This marked the end of what had been an extremely successful partnership between Monnet and French Foreign Minister Schuman. But Monnet had not given up on European integration just yet. In the Belgian prime minister Paul Henri Spaak, he found an important new ally to pursue the goal of a federal Europe. At an ECSC meeting in the Italian resort of Messina, Monnet and Spaak restarted the European project through the establishment of a committee, chaired by Spaak, that would investigate the possibility of further integration in other areas. The support of the six ECSC member states to set up such a committee was an indication that, despite the failures of the EDC, a strong desire remained to pursue the European project.

The member states were relatively noncommittal at the conference and left Spaak a degree of flexibility as to how the process of integration should be pursued. Spaak seized this opportunity by arguing for the integration of the European atomic industry in an organization to be called EURATOM (European Atomic Energy Community).[4] In addition to the original six, EURATOM also envisioned the inclusion of Britain, and representatives from London were invited to attend the meeting at Messina. But the UK wanted only very limited integration in the form of a free trade area. Such a position was untenable in the view of the other states, and the UK left the Messina conference before it had even finished, thereby leaving Britain with only a peripheral role in the European project.

But although an agreement on atomic industry was reached, economic integration was more problematic. France, in particular, still feared the emerging industrial and economic might of its historical enemy, Germany. The French government insisted that a sudden exposure of the country's industrial sector to the competitive forces of a European market would be catastrophic for France's economic growth and employment. In the end, French acceptance of the common market was secured by creating a Common Agricultural Policy (CAP) from which France would reap substantial benefits.

Given the disproportionate political power that the agricultural sector wielded in the French National Assembly, the CAP proposition seemed too good to miss. The introduction of the CAP in the proposed European Economic Community (EEC) Treaty therefore strongly contributed to the acceptance of the Treaty in France, but the accord was also welcomed by agricultural interests in other member states.

The Treaties of Rome, signed in March 1957, established the EEC and EURATOM. The EEC Treaty was the more significant of the two in both content and structure, and its principles were extremely ambitious. Article 2 stated that the EEC would "promote throughout the Community a harmonious development of economic activities, a continuous and balanced expansion, an increase in stability, an accelerated raising of the standard of living and closer relations between the states belonging to it." This statement made it clear that the EEC would not remain simply a loose, consultative economic forum. On the contrary, the EEC Treaty provided core principles that would form the basis for the extension of its powers in the future. In particular, the establishment of the European Common Market (ECM) was envisioned to be achieved through the realization of the four economic freedoms: the free movement of goods, capital, services, and persons across borders and beyond national regulations.[5]

The Intergovernmental Assertion of the 1960s

The optimism that surrounded the European project was bolstered by Europe's rapid economic growth between the 1950s and the early 1960s. Between 1955 and 1964, for example, West Germany's GDP rose by 40.3 percent. Against this backdrop of progress in Rome in 1957 and in Paris in 1951, the first strong challenge to the European integration project came as a surprise. The political figure central to these developments was the French president Charles de Gaulle. De Gaulle's leading role in organizing the resistance movement against Nazi-occupied France had given him the status of a national hero and subsequently propelled him to the French presidency of the Fifth Republic in December 1958. De Gaulle was not anti-Europe and, in fact, had supported the EEC early in his presidency, most notably the establishment of the CAP. Nonetheless, de Gaulle was willing to challenge the smooth progress of European integration by blocking Britain's first EEC membership application in 1963, arguing that the UK did not have a true "European vocation" and was, in fact, merely an "American Trojan horse," meaning that Britain would simply act as a champion of U.S. government policy.[6]

By 1967 de Gaulle's attitude toward the UK had not changed, and once again he vetoed Britain's second application to the EEC, citing the same reasons that he had four years earlier. De Gaulle was also skeptical of any institutional developments that might undermine the national sovereignty of France. For him, a union—whether political or purely economic—was only viable if the national interests of the member states could be safeguarded at all times. It is safe to say that de Gaulle personified the intergovernmentalists.

De Gaulle found a further nemesis in Walter Hallstein, the acting president of the European Commission.[7] Hallstein thought that it would be only appropriate for the EEC, as a union of democracies, to introduce some form of majority voting in its institutions, and, in particular, in the Council of Ministers. De Gaulle opposed majority rule, even though the Treaty of Rome had provided for its introduction at the end of a transitional period. But de Gaulle was extremely critical of this idea, as this would open the gate for a majority of countries being able to overrule France, should it be in the minority. Hallstein's idea also would have strengthened the position of the supranational European Commission, as proposals by this institution would have required the majority of member states to oppose it.

To protest Hallstein's proposition, de Gaulle recalled all French ministers from Brussels, resulting in the "empty chair crisis," which started in mid-1965 and continued until the summit meeting in Luxembourg of all European partners in January 1966. The term "crisis" was justified, since any proposals within the EEC required the unanimous support of all six member states. The summit in Luxembourg reached a compromise (the "Luxembourg Compromise") which resolved that,

> Where, in the case of decisions which may be taken by majority vote on a proposal from the Commission, very important interests of one or more of the member states are at stake, the Members of the Council will endeavor, within a reasonable time, to reach solutions which can be adopted by all the Members of the Council while respecting the mutual interests and those of the Community.

The member states therefore had agreed in principle to a system of majority voting. But if, at any stage, a member state felt that its national interest might be threatened, the voting would simply switch back to unanimity. The logical outcome of this was that unanimous voting remained the norm, but at least the European partners in principle agreed to advance their cooperation in a supranational manner through majority voting. Also, any single country could still veto a proposal by the European Commission. This meant that the pace of European integration was now firmly controlled by member states. The empty chair crisis may have been removed, but the compromise reached had a far-reaching impact, fundamentally altering the delicate balance of powers between the Commission and the member states that had been built into the treaties of Rome and Paris.

The Political Spring of 1969: The Hague Summit

Throughout the Western world, the 1960s witnessed far-reaching social and political changes. In the United States, the Civil Rights movement, the murders of the Kennedy brothers and Martin Luther King, as well as growing resentment and protest over the country's involvement in the Vietnam War led to antagonistic and occasionally explosive political discourse, in marked contrast to the comparatively harmonious 1950s. In the U.S., widespread student protests against the Vietnam War in the spring of 1968 vividly demonstrated that a new political dawn was on the horizon. From London to Amsterdam, Berlin, and Paris, younger generations grew increasingly critical of the political elites of the 1960s who, some felt, represented a former era more closely associated with World War II.[8] But the turbulent events of the 1960s also helped to reignite the dormant European project. The initial impetus came from France itself. The student upheavals of 1968 had also seriously damaged the French economy, forcing a devaluation of the franc. After ten years in office de Gaulle resigned and was replaced by George Pompidou, a long-standing member of the Gaullist party, who nevertheless had little desire to challenge the integration process. Given the state of his country's economy, Pompidou saw the economic welfare of France inextricably linked to the EEC. A further contributing factor was the emergence of West Germany as Europe's economic powerhouse,[9] raising concerns over that country's potential economic domination over its European partners. Finally, the EEC had emerged as a highly attractive vehicle for organizing Europe and, in addition to the UK, Denmark and Ireland became increasingly impatient to join the community.

In the end, the summit in The Hague addressed three major issues concerning integration that can be summarized as "deepening, widening, and completing." "Deepening" investigated the possibility of cooperation in the field of foreign policy. More important, deepening referred in particular to West Germany; given this country's economic might, the European leaders agreed to look further into the possibility of an economic and monetary union, including a single European currency, that could integrate the German economy more effectively into a wider European setting. The goal was to prevent the West German government, and the monetary policies of its independent central bank, the *Bundesbank*, from having detrimental consequences for other countries.[10]

"Widening" simply referred to accepting Denmark, Great Britain, and Ireland as new member states. Accession of the three countries was completed in 1973. "Completing" forced the European Community,[11] as it was then called, to look closely at past treaty achievements and to assess whether these had been put into practice. In particular, the establishment of a European Common Market, which had been a goal of the Treaty of Rome in 1957, when it established the free movement of goods, services, capital, and people, was still far from a political and economic reality and instead was obstructed by different national regulations and standards.

Still and all, the summit in The Hague offered a brief window of supranationalism after an intergovernmental interlude dominated by the Luxembourg Compromise. The principles of deepening, widening, and completing indeed represented a bold agenda: to propel the European Community further, with new members and new policies based on a more solid and coherent foundation.

The Eurosclerosis of the 1970s

The term "sclerosis" refers to a medical condition involving constrictive processes that hinder movement, and indeed, after the optimism surrounding The Hague Summit, in the 1970s the member states paid little attention to European integration or to finding common solutions to shared problems. The early 1970s, moreover, were indeed tumultuous internationally. U.S. President Richard Nixon abandoned the Bretton Woods system, which, since its inception in 1944, had provided for fixed exchange rates. Nixon argued that the dollar was overvalued and that a freely traded U.S. currency would boost American exports. Nixon was right, as West European currencies, most notably the British pound and the German Deutschmark, rose in value relative to the dollar. In addition, Libya's leader, Colonel Muammar Gaddhafi, in 1973, convinced his fellow Arab leaders to decrease the production of oil. The Organization of the Petroleum Exporting Countries (OPEC) repeated the trick again in 1979, and on both occasions the costs for Western businesses and consumers increased significantly.

The first oil crisis, combined with the effects of the dollar crisis of 1971, plunged Western European economies into a recession, albeit by today's standard a relatively mild one. The unemployment rate of Europe's biggest economy, West Germany, rose from 1 percent in early 1973 to a high of 5.1 percent in August 1975. Ever since the early 1950s, Western Europe gradually had become accustomed to continuous economic growth. Over nearly the previous twenty-five years, Western Europeans were safe in the knowledge that every year the economic well-being of their societies was improving. In light of this comfortable state of mind, the downturn of the 1970s was a shock that caused widespread concern.

After the euphoria of 1969, one might have assumed that the European Community would seek common solutions to common problems. After all, every member state was affected by the fall of the U.S. dollar, the rise of the price of oil, and the subsequent economic recession. The culmination of the dollar crisis in 1971 forced the EC to consider how its national economies could operate without the stability in exchange rates that was guaranteed by linkage to the U.S. dollar. The relevance of economic and monetary cooperation, and even the introduction of a European single currency, were all of a sudden much more relevant. But attempts to create an Economic and Monetary Union (EMU) were disbanded by 1973, to be replaced by a much looser commitment that merely asked national governments to keep the values of their currencies within a narrow range of one another.[12] The Werner Committee, which had been set up to assess the possibility of European monetary integration, was faced with an array of obstacles. The Committee stated that the institutional implications of enlargement were inextricably linked to institutional reform in the EC. For reasons of democratic legitimacy, Werner argued that the creation of a European Central Bank—a key requirement for EMU—would have to be accountable to the European Parliament. But such a sweeping institutional reform was just too much for an already overloaded agenda that included the pressures of integrating Denmark, Ireland, and the United Kingdom. In addition, there were already many different conflicting ideas about the larger problem of merging the national economies into a single European one, and the member states could not agree on the EMU project.

Thus, even beyond the ambitious EMU, the advancement of the overall European project came to a sudden standstill. Although the OPEC crisis triggered economic recession across the EC, the member states had little incentive to promote economic cooperation on a European level, since each state was struggling to maintain its own economic prosperity. This shortsightedness limited the scope for developing longer-term strategies or more ambitious projects to merely symbolic gestures of protracted negotiations. The inability of the European Commission to provide leadership in this environment led to summit meetings in the informal but highly influential European Council. The French president Giscard d'Estaing, who had replaced Pompidou in 1974, launched informal summit meetings in 1975, thereby further increasing the role of the member states in the policy-making process. Just as the Luxembourg Compromise had limited the role of the European Commission in advancing integration through specific policy proposals, now the evolution of summitry undermined the Commission's role in setting the strategic agenda.

Another strain on progress toward integration was the accession of the UK. After two previous failures, British Prime Minister Edward Heath had been keen to ensure that this time the UK would join successfully. His attitude can be summed up as "get in now, worry about the problems later," a tactic that would keep the European Community busy solving the problems for years to come. The question of the UK's financial contributions, for example, caused much controversy. The EC spent a great deal of its budget on agriculture, so even though farming had relatively little importance in the UK, accession made that country the second biggest net contributor. Although a new regional policy aimed at developing poorer areas somewhat compensated Britain for the lack of subsidies it received from the EC's agricultural policy, the issue of UK contributions would provide ammunition for anti-European politicians in the UK well into the next decade.

Although the European Court of Justice made some important decisions during the 1970s, the decade was dominated by member-state politics, a policy-making system that was paralyzed by its own complexity and the inability of the main actors to develop sufficient momentum to launch new policy initiatives. The term "sclerosis," the inability to move, is therefore an apt term to describe the European condition at this time.

A New Direction for European Integration in the 1980s

After the inactivity of the 1970s, the dawn of a new decade coincided with internal and external developments that reinvigorated the European project. Japan and the United States were about to embark on a period of significant economic growth, which forced European leaders to streamline their markets in order to improve their international competitiveness.[13] The 1980s also saw a further round of enlargement of the European Community. Three former fascist dictatorships—Portugal, Spain, and Greece—all sought to anchor their young democracies within a community of stable political systems. Despite the weak economic infrastructure of Greece, that country's accession in 1981 was handled quite speedily. A little more difficult was the accession of the two Iberian candidates. Specifically, negotiations over Spain's membership were complicated by concerns expressed in Italy and France, which offered the same agricultural products as Spain and feared a significant drop in income for their own farmers once Spanish competitors were also allowed to offer their produce to European consumers. Not until 1986 did Portugal and Spain join the Community. But despite some difficult negotiations, this southern expansion confirmed that the EC had established itself as a highly attractive vehicle for organizing Europe.

Another reinvigorating development was that much needed institutional reforms had started to have an impact on the European scene. For the first time, direct elections were held to the European Parliament in 1979. Although this institution was included in the Treaty of Rome, Members of the European Parliament (MEPs) were previously appointed by national governments. Although 1979 did not see increased powers for Parliament, which only had an advisory legislative function, it did have two important effects. First, it gave a much-needed degree of legitimacy to the European Community that had been lacking before. This in turn attracted political actors who had previously not found Parliament an attractive proposition. New people with greater political ambitions and capabilities gave the Community a new dynamic and added a further source of political pressure to reinvigorate the European project.

On another internal level, in 1979 we saw the arrival of UK Prime Minister Margaret Thatcher, who, as a neo-liberal, saw the grand opportunity that a more unified European market could offer Britain. After all, it is more profitable to sell one's products to potentially 340 million European consumers than to only 60 million Brits. Like her counterpart Ronald Reagan, she was an advocate of neo-liberal policies and pursued an intensive privatization program. Companies in which the British government had at least part ownership were sold to the public sector, including British Airways and British Telecom. Thatcher was also adamant about keeping the UK's budget under tight monetary control, resulting in drastic cuts in welfare spending. She was often portrayed as the "Euroskeptic" par excellence. It is true that her abrasive confrontational style often did not go down too well with her European partners. She criticized European institutions for being too bureaucratic and costly, and she passionately fought many proposals that might have undermined British national sovereignty. But the image of the feisty lady, banging her handbag on the negotiating tables of Brussels, ought to be at least slightly rectified. As a politician who advocated the principle of the free market, an enlarged European free market was too good an opportunity to let pass.

All these internal and external factors were conducive to a change in direction. Now it fell to the leader of the European bureaucracy, the Commission President Jacques Delors, to elevate the Community to a new level, which he did by spurring the implementation of the Single European Market (SEM)—the free movement of goods, services, capital, and labor—through precise steps. Delors had been the finance minister of France under a socialist government, and he combined three unique qualities which, taken by themselves, would already have been quite impressive. First, he was a cunning diplomat and negotiator, always well prepared and briefed before summit meetings. Delors often managed to forge alliances behind people's backs, and he had a proactive control of the EC's agenda and more than once acted as the masterful puppet player who controlled the European heads of government. His clashes with Thatcher became the stuff of legends.

Second, Delors was a very skilful bureaucrat. Based on an in-depth report by Delors' fellow commissioner, Lord Cockfield, in 1985, the Community agreed to finally realize the single market, which had already been agreed to thirty years earlier with the Treaty of Rome. Delors however, turned that theoretical objective into practical reality by drafting 270 precise measures, which, once implemented by the member states, would guarantee the four freedoms. Delors even had the courage to impose a six-year deadline on the implementation, after which the member states would be subject to fines by the European Commission. An especially impressive feature of the Cockfield report was a timetable that was not only realistic but also sufficiently transparent to ensure that the necessary pressure from the Commission could be maintained. Lastly, Delors was a visionary who adopted a commonsensical approach to the future of the European project, and questioned which policies would have been better organized at the supranational rather than the national level. For instance, the environment is essentially supranational; clouds and rivers, and therefore pollution, do not recognize borders. With this fact in mind, Delors was able to convince national leaders to set up a European environmental policy. Further evidence that supranational efforts were needed was provided by the technological innovations emanating from Japan and the United States; because individual European countries were unable to keep pace with those countries in these areas, Delors argued for transnational cooperation in scientific research and technology—this ultimately resulted, for instance, in the development of the Airbus.

The Single European Act

The Single European Act (SEA), signed by the member states in 1986, marked a dramatic departure from the intergovernmentalism that dominated the previous seventeen years. At last, the spirit of The Hague, in 1969, resulted in concrete treaty commitments. The SEA linked the re-launching of European integration with institutional reform and a range of new policy responsibilities, a strategy that would maintain the momentum of the invigorated European Community for years to

Table 1.4. The Single European Act (1986)

New policies:
- Research and Technology
- Single Market Deadline for 1992
- European Political Cooperation

Institutional reform:
- more power to the EP
- qualified majority voting

---

come. The key characteristics of the SEA can be seen in terms of the policy areas and institutional reforms and their political consequences.

The main policy area of the SEA was the Single European Market initiative, with its famous 1992 deadline, which reasserted the free movement of goods, services, capital, and labor, and of course meant the removal of national quotas and tariffs. However, the SEM went further than any previous attempts at establishing a single European market. This time, the SEM was concerned with removing non-tariff barriers that distorted trade through different product specifications or purchasing agreements. This would finally secure the four freedoms outlined in the Treaty of Rome. In addition, completely new policy areas involved cohesion (the reduction of economic and social inequalities between rich and poor regions), research and technology, and European Political Co-operation (EPC), a forum to discuss foreign policy. The Single European Act, with its SEM Initiative and impressive range of new policy fields, certainly moved toward accomplishing the two key goals of completing and deepening, which had been the objective of The Hague summit of 1969.

The main elements of institutional reform were primarily concerned with the introduction of a system of majority voting. Though majority voting was initially restricted to issues connected to the completion of the Single European Market, it nonetheless represented a significant departure from an era dominated by the Luxembourg Compromise. It also significantly increased the status of the EC's bureaucratic apparatus (the European Commission), because individual member states were no longer able to block single-handedly legislative proposals emanating from that organization. Second, the role of the European Parliament was increased. Although members of the EP had been directly elected since 1979, their legislative function was severely curtailed, given that they were only consulted once the Commission had already drafted and proposed new laws. The SEA, however, introduced a new procedure[14] through which the EP was now allowed to play a role in amending legislation, albeit only on a limited number of issues. In addition, another procedure[15] required the approval of a majority of MEPs in cases where the European Community incorporated new member states or concluded international agreements. Though the powers of the EP still paled in comparison with other democratic assemblies, the SEA nonetheless was seen as an important improvement in the democratic features of the Community.

The political consequences were also significant, as the existence of the SEA demonstrated that Europe was now an important area of real political activity. The interaction between national ministries and departments, on the one hand, and the European bureaucracy in Brussels, on the other, had intensified as new legislative proposals drafted by the Commission ran their course. Also, with the rise of the SEM, interest groups began to pay more attention, and subsequently the number of lobby groups present in Brussels skyrocketed. Finally, the SEA created the largest and wealthiest market in the world, and it gave the Community a much greater weight at the international level. In particular, the Uruguay Round, which started in 1986 and aimed to set up global free trade, was heavily influenced by the Europeans who negotiated as a single, unified economic actor.

A New World Order in the 1990s

Throughout the history of European integration, internal reforms often were the political responses to major external events. By far the most important event was the collapse of communism in Central and Eastern Europe between 1989 and 1991. One by one, the former communist satellite states of Hungary, Czechoslovakia, Poland, Romania, Bulgaria, and East Germany shed their authoritarian past and held free elections. Nascent democratic regimes in these states sought closer cooperation with the rest of Europe. In December 1991 the old Soviet Union ceased to exist and was replaced by a loose so-called Commonwealth of Independent States (CIS). These political developments posed severe challenges for the European Community. With the old Warsaw Pact gone, a security vacuum emerged, and no one could safely predict whether the transitions to democracy and capitalism in Central and Eastern Europe would be successful. The worst-case scenario could have been a return to autocratic forms of government. Furthermore, after years of communist rule, democratic practices and institutions, as well as a pluralistic civil society, needed to be established in countries with little or no history of democracy. Hence Western European states had to prepare themselves for such possible security threats as drugs and human trafficking, organized crime, or widespread migratory movements, and to seek institutional mechanisms to address these problems.

The collapse of communism, however, also brought more immediate concerns for the Community in the shape of German unification. In economic terms, the fall of the Berlin Wall resulted in the unification of the West European champion and the champion of the communist trading bloc, the Council for Mutual Economic Assistance, or COMECON. Despite both the significant financial costs of unification and the run-down state of the East German industrial infrastructure, European leaders, most notably French President François Mitterrand, felt that an already economically dominant West Germany would become even more capable of further dominating the European economy. Mitterrand saw further European integration as a safeguard against such dominance, and he strongly pushed for closer economic and monetary integration.

It therefore came as no surprise that, only five years after the SEA, the Community embarked on another amendment to its treaties. But in the run-up to the summit in the Dutch town of Maastricht in December 1991, a number of opposing views on the future direction of European integration began to swell the political agenda. Arguing for a more supranational path, Commission President Jacques Delors published a report in 1989 on the benefits of economic and monetary union. In a similar vein, the report by Commissioner Cecchini, in 1988, had analyzed the costs of what he called a non-Europe that would fail to integrate to greater degrees. Margaret Thatcher, meanwhile, was increasingly skeptical of the ambitions of the Brussels bureaucracy, and in her famous speech at the College of Europe in Bruges in 1988 she refocused the debate on the limits of European integration by arguing for the safeguarding of national sovereignty and independence.[16] She stressed that "willing and active cooperation between independent and sovereign states is the best way to build a European Community."

Disagreement over the precise path of future integration among the European political elite was now mirrored by the public. For a treaty to be ratified, each member state had to approve of it; depending on national constitutional requirements, this could be done either by a parliamentary act (the most common form) or by referendum (as used, for instance, in Denmark and Ireland). After finally agreeing on the Maastricht Treaty—officially called the Treaty on the European Union—Mitterrand decided to hold a referendum, even though ratification by the French parliament would have been sufficient. Mitterrand argued that the popular approval, which a clearly won referendum could offer, would carry more symbolic weight and would encourage ratification in other countries. There was one flaw in his calculation, however; until the 1990s European integration was largely an elitist project, with only rare interaction between politicians and the general public. The policies of the Single European Act of 1986 with its establishment of the Single Market and to an even greater extent the policies of this new Treaty with its proposed introduction of a single currency had a much more tangible effect on the lives of European citizens. Many reacted with skepticism, borne not necessarily out of opposition to the European idea but simply out of a lack of information. The referendum in France just produced a "yes" vote by the narrowest of margins. With a 70 percent turnout in September 1992, the referendum was approved by only 51 percent. Thus instead of an affirmation of France's pro-European stance, the referendum turned into a disastrous public relations exercise.

In Denmark, ratification of the Maastricht Treaty was rejected outright in a referendum in June 1992. Obviously the entire ratification process was in jeopardy. The Danish government therefore negotiated an opt-out clause for Maastricht's most controversial policy—the single European currency—and at another referendum, in May 1993, the Danes finally gave their approval.

Britain experienced similar political turmoil when John Major, who replaced Thatcher as prime minister in 1990, decided not to hold a referendum. The parliamentary act of approval turned out to be a troublesome affair that split his ruling Conservative Party. Major was also forced to negotiate an opt-out clause both for the single currency and for the social charter that established certain workers' rights throughout Europe. In the end, only a watered-down version of the treaty for the UK and Denmark placed the ratification train back on track.

The Treaty on the European Union (Maastricht Treaty)

Against the backdrop of these conflicts over the future of European integration, the Treaty on the European Union (TEU) represented a compromise that was actually less coherent than the previous SEA treaty of 1986. Of course, responses needed to be found to new internal and external challenges, but these had to finely balance intergovernmental concerns over a potential loss of the member states' national sovereignty and supranational aspirations for an increasingly unified Europe.

The TEU was unique and far-reaching in content and structure. First, the European Community gave itself a new name—the European Union—reflecting the closer nature of the member states' relationships with one another. The TEU also referred for the first time to citizenship values and gave Europeans, at least those who were citizens of an EU member state, uniform rights. This attempt to address the Union's lack of democratic credibility was complemented by a number of institutional innovations. The legislative powers of the European Parliament were increased through a new method for drafting legislation called the co-decision procedure.[17] The EP was also told to appoint an ombudsperson so that EU citizens could challenge administrative decisions taken by any EU institution. Another independent institution—the Committee of the Regions—was created to include sub-national, regional voices in the EU's legislative process; this Committee had to be consulted whenever a regional issue appeared on the agenda.

Even more significant, the TEU completely elevated new policy fields to the European level, away from the exclusive authority of the member states. Although the TEU did not replace previous treaties but only amended them, these amendments were indeed far-reaching. The TEU was organized as three pillars. First and foremost was pillar I, also called the Economic Community, containing previous treaties and their revisions but also important new policies, most notably the single currency and EMU. The second pillar introduced a Common Foreign and Security Policy (CFSP). The third addressed cooperation in the fields of Justice and Home Affairs (JHA), including such issues as police cooperation, immigration, asylum, and internal security matters. The most important difference between the three pillars was that decisions in pillars II (CFSP) and III (JHA) would be made through intergovernmental negotiations between member states, whereas the largely economic pillar I retained and extended supranational policy making.

Table 1.5. The Maastricht Treaty (1992)

Pillar I Economic Community	Pillar II Common Foreign and Security Policy	Pillar III Justice and Home Affairs
Economic and Monetary Union Single Market	Unified International diplomacy Common Defence Policy	Asylum, immigration Police cooperation, customs
Qualified Majority Voting	Unanimous Agreements	Unanimous Agreements
Supranationalism	Intergovernmentalism	Intergovernmentalism

The most significant innovation was, undoubtedly, the decision to merge national macroeconomic policies in an Economic and Monetary Union. Essentially EMU envisaged not only a single currency but also a single monetary policy, such as one interest rate, for all participating countries. Obviously EMU would relieve companies trading across borders and cross-border travelers the cost of exchanging currencies. This also meant that national central banks could no longer fine-tune their economies by adjusting interest rates in response to changing economic climates. In the Maastricht Treaty, the member states agreed both to a timetable for implementing EMU by 1999 and to a number of European institutions to manage the transition.

The CFSP of pillar II provided a framework enabling member states to present a unified presence in international diplomacy. Because foreign and security policy are often regarded as vital bastions of a country's national sovereignty, this was indeed a very ambitious undertaking. It bears repeating that joint diplomatic action was not based on majority voting but on unanimous agreement by all member states, which greatly reduced the scope of diplomacy. As was seen in the Iraq crisis in the spring of 2003, EU member states could not agree on a common approach to dealing with Saddam Hussein, which simply meant that on that occasion one could not speak of a common policy response. Finally, the CFSP built a framework for developing a common defense policy through the Western European Union (WEU)[18] that would "elaborate and implement decisions and actions of the Union which have defense implications" (Article J4 TEU).

The third pillar, representing Justice and Home Affairs, provided guidelines for coordinating various ad hoc arrangements concerning asylum, drug trafficking, or customs. As with pillar II, the CFSP, JHA offered member states a chance to develop joint actions in these fields but, again, only through unanimity.

Without question, the institutional reforms and policy innovations dramatically changed the face of the European project. But this push for closer integration came at a high price. Because of severe public concern in Denmark and Britain, the ratification process could only be safeguarded by offering these countries the option to withdraw from EMU (Denmark and Britain) and from the social charter (Britain only).[19] As a result, the notion of European solidarity, of a one-size-fits-all Europe, was now gone. Instead, Maastricht introduced the concept of a Europe à la carte—albeit in a mild form—where member states rejected policies that were not in line with their own national political agenda. The provision of the opt-out clauses accommodated differences between member states, and thus highlighted the serious differences between European governments concerning the future of the EU.

Another result was that the European project turned from an elitist undertaking driven by individual political leaders into a hotly debated issue that was now part of the political mainstream. The referenda in France and Denmark offered ample evidence for this. In the UK, the Maastricht debate had split the ruling Conservative Party, as well as the public. In Germany, often portrayed as one of the continent's main driving forces for European integration, the general population harbored serious doubts over whether it was a good idea to give up their beloved Deutschmark for some supranational coins and notes. The responses by European citizens to the Maastricht Treaty effectively placed a limit on the speed and extent of integration that the populace of the member states would tolerate. Any further treaty amendments therefore had to be less ambitious and more intent on ironing out some of the institutional and policy shortcomings that still undermined the Union.

The Treaty of Amsterdam

The Amsterdam Treaty, agreed to by the EU's political leaders on 17 June 1997 and signed on 2 October of that year, was the culmination of two years of discussions and negotiations about the goal of a citizens' Europe, the role of the European Union on the international stage, improvements in the institutions' operations, and the prospect of enlarging the Union. Specific issues addressed were economic globalization and its impact on jobs, the fight against terrorism, international crime and drug trafficking, ecological problems, and threats to public health. The Treaty finally entered into force in April 1999.

A few years earlier, in 1995, the Union had welcomed three more members: Austria, Finland, and Sweden, which had been neutral countries, siding neither with NATO nor the Warsaw Pact. But with the demise of the latter, the rationale for staying outside the EU was no longer valid. The existing EU hugely welcomed this expansion of its club, which was not surprising given the prosperity levels of the candidates, which added much needed funds to the Union's coffers. Specifically, the Amsterdam Treaty focused on fundamental rights such as gender equality, non-discrimination, and data privacy. It included a new section on visas, asylum, and immigration, as well as police and judicial cooperation in criminal matters. The free movement of people was considerably strengthened by the decision to integrate the previously bilateral Schengen Agreement, which abolished border controls between signatory countries.[20]

Table 1.6. The Treaty of Amsterdam (1997)

- Four Objectives
  - putting employment and citizen's rights at the heart of the EU
  - moving freely and living in a secure environment
  - giving Europe a voice in the world
  - creating effective institutions for an enlarged Europe
- Achieving the Objectives
  - Schengen Agreement incorporated in the treaty
  - Cooperation between police forces and customs
  - Coordinated strategy for employment
  - High Representative for Common Foreign and Security Policy

---

The Treaty of Amsterdam brought much needed clarification of the concept of European citizenship.[21] It also included a chapter on the coordination of national employment policies, as well as emphasizing a stronger commitment to tackle social exclusion. Further, four years after Maastricht had introduced CFSP, the Amsterdam treaty established the post of High Representative to give the EU's foreign policy greater prominence and coherence. As for institutional reforms, the treaty gave the European Parliament a considerable boost by broadening the use of the co-decision procedure in which the EP had a veto power on all legislative proposals. After the crisis over the ratification of Maastricht, the EU clearly tried to use the Amsterdam treaty to win over Europe's citizens through four prime measures:

- placing employment and citizens' rights at the heart of the Union,
- allowing Europeans to move freely and live in a secure environment
- giving Europe a message and a voice in the world
- providing effective institutions for an enlarged EU

But this ambitious public-relations exercise had a mixed reception. As in the case of EMU, the bilateral Schengen Agreement again granted opt-outs for the UK, Ireland, and Denmark, thereby creating further asymmetry within the EU. Also, the post of High Representative for the CFSP, which was occupied by the Spaniard Javier Solana, did not give the EU the expected stronger voice in the world. With several members of the European Commission already active on the international stage (most notably the commissioners responsible for trade, agriculture, external relations, and enlargement), this new post only raised a puzzling question: Who represents the EU abroad? Furthermore, a coordinated strategy on employment may have sounded laudable, but such promises were dismissed as impractical given the increasing pressures of globalization to which Europe's economies had to adjust as well as the neo-liberal approaches of a number of EU member states. Finally, the treaty did not create the institutions needed to integrate the former communist countries of Central and Eastern Europe. The EU itself acknowledged that the reforms were merely a step toward more effective institutions but were not the ultimate answer. Institutional questions, therefore, were subsequently addressed more vigorously during the next round of negotiations that culminated in the Treaty of Nice (see below). Nonetheless, the concept of a European citizenship and the (albeit limited) integration of fundamental rights principles gave the EU a new direction; the EU was now headed toward a more coherent and complete polity that significantly departed from the mainly economic outlook of the Rome and Paris treaties.

The Treaty of Nice

The third treaty amendment in the space of less than ten years (and the fourth amendment since the Eurosclerosis of the 1970s) was negotiated in Nice in December 2000. Under the chairmanship of the French president Jacques Chirac, the member states devoted this summit to preparing the Union for the challenges of enlargement. Thus, institutional and democratic reform were high on the agenda.

European leaders recognized that the composition and responsibilities of the EU institutions that had been adopted in the 1950s by the six founding member states had become outdated by 2000, when the EU was about to expand to twenty-seven members.[22] Yet, apart from the introduction of direct elections to the European Parliament in 1979, there had been no major institutional reform. Clearly, in Nice, the old EU-15 realized that the organization was in much need of major institutional reform. The Intergovernmental Conference (IGC),[23] which preceded the Nice meeting, had to come up with a vision of how the Union could function effectively with an expanded membership. Without going into too much detail,[24] Nice limited the size of the European Parliament to 732 members, while also placing a ceiling on the number of commissioners (a maximum of 27). After acrimonious and lengthy negotiations, the summit also agreed to a new voting formula for the Council of Ministers, which acts as the intergovernmental forum of the member states with the main responsibility of approving legislation. Apart from these institutional changes, the EU also tried to silence its critics by addressing democratic shortcomings, specifically the lack of a fundamental rights agenda.

Prior to the Nice Summit, a group of constitutional experts had drafted a Charter on Fundamental Rights and recommended that it be included in the EU treaty structure. The Charter sets out the civil, political, economic, and social rights of EU citizens under six headings: dignity, freedom, equality, solidarity, citizens' rights, and justice. These rights were based on the fundamental rights and freedoms recognized by the European Convention for the Protection of Human Rights and Fundamental Freedoms, as well as on the constitutional traditions of EU countries.

Although the Charter was viewed favorably by most member states, UK Prime Minister Tony Blair refused to permit the Charter to be enforceable under EU law or to allow the European Court of Justice to base its rulings on it. Nonetheless, the EU

Table 1.7. The Treaty of Nice (2001)

- Changes
  1. European Parliament: capped at 732 MEPs
  2. Council of Ministers: more policies will be decided under majority voting by using a new voting system
  3. Commission: capped at 27 members
  4. Commission President can fire commissioners and change their portfolios
- Aspects not Addressed
  1. Fundamental Rights Charter still not part of EU law
  2. Unanimity voting remains in such policy areas as tax, cohesion, CFSP, JHA

---

took significant steps to address undemocratic practices. Prompted by Austria's far-right Freedom Party becoming a coalition partner in the Austrian government, and by the subsequent wave of Austria's diplomatic isolation, the EU adopted a clear procedure on how to deal with member states that departed from the democratic track. The Council of Ministers, with a majority comprised of four-fifths of its members, and with the approval of the European Parliament, could now declare that a clear danger existed of a member state committing a serious breach of the fundamental rights or freedoms on which the Union was founded. The Council could then issue "appropriate recommendations" to that member state, although Nice explicitly shied away from allowing a member state to be expelled from the Union.

Nonetheless, given the daunting challenge of extending the Nice Treaty into Central and Eastern Europe, the treaty could not be considered a success. President Jacques Chirac, as the leader of the host country, was severely criticized for insufficiently organizing the summit, and his forceful, if not arrogant, approach to diplomacy caused much consternation in London, Berlin, and other European capitals. First, the haggling over the specific voting majorities in the Council of Ministers caused frustration, prompting critics to describe it as a bargaining approach more suited to a flea market than to intergovernmental decision making. Second, the exclusion of the Human Rights Charter from enforceable EU law further emphasized that the EU was primarily an economic union, with only secondary interest in political and social rights. Third, calls for a clearer delineation of power between member states and Brussels, and between national parliaments and the European Parliament were not addressed. Finally, it seemed doubtful whether the Nice summit prepared the EU sufficiently for expansion. Important issues that were not addressed included the budget and, above all, reform of the financially wasteful agricultural policy. Such crucial matters were postponed to another IGC that would then include representatives from the ten new member states that joined in 2004.

Quo Vadis EU: The Road to the Reform Treaty of 2007

An important step toward reforming the EU, especially its institutions, would have been the ratification of a constitution. Over eighteen months between 2002 and 2003, the so-called Convention for Europe[25] managed to draft a supposed Constitution for Europe. Representatives at the Convention were drawn from a wide range of backgrounds, including national and EU parliamentarians, members of civil society, and government representatives. For this draft to become EU law, ratification by every member state would have been necessary. In most countries, this would have been done through simple parliamentary approval, but others decided to hold a referendum on the issue. The initial text put forward by the Convention did not meet the approval of Spain and Poland, since both benefited greatly from the Treaty of Nice which gave them disproportionately powerful voting rights in the Council of Ministers. Italy's prime minister, Silvio Berlusconi, whose government had the presidency of the EU in the second half of 2003, failed to agree on a compromise, and it was up to Berlusconi's successor, Irish Prime Minister Bertie Ahern, to pick up the pieces. After some acrimonious debates, during which Jacques Chirac and Tony Blair clashed on several points, a compromise was reached.

Alas, negative referenda in France and the Netherlands in May 2005 meant that this treaty revision did not become effective. Chris Patten, former Commissioner for External Relations (1999–2004), described the constitutional process as "dead as a dodo." But this did not mean that the EU was without any legal foundation, as it simply continued to rely on the Treaty of Nice and the decisions reached there. With the accession of Bulgaria and Romania in 2007, calls for institutional reforms again were voiced from several member states. Indeed, the underlying rationale had not changed but instead had become even more precarious: an institutional set up designed for six countries in the 1950s could hardly cope with the political reality of an ever expanding club now comprised of twenty-seven members.

During the German presidency in the first half of 2007, Chancellor Angela Merkel was pressing for a new treaty before the EU could even contemplate further enlargement rounds. At a summit meeting in June 2007 the EU agreed on a new treaty; though it was called a Reform Treaty (or Lisbon Treaty, based on the capital where the treaty was signed in December 2007), it was actually a stripped-down version of the Constitution (a term, incidentally, that was dropped altogether) and contained some of the improvements already envisioned by the proposed Constitution. As with all the other treaties, this new agreement is subject to approval by all member states. But a negative referendum in Ireland in June 2008 posed a severe doubt over the ratification process. At the time of this writing, it is impossible to predict which aspects of the Reform Treaty will be taken on board. The main changes to the EU are the following:

1. A system of double majority voting in the Council of Ministers, so that decisions require the approval of 55 percent of the member states which must represent at least 65 percent of the EU population. This new voting configuration however, will not take effect until 2014.
2. A legally binding Charter of Fundamental Rights.
3. The appointment of an EU High Representative for the Common Foreign and Security Policy, located within the European Commission and therefore supported by a larger staff.
4. A full-time president who will chair the European Council (i.e., the summit meetings of heads of government) for two and a half years.
5. The strengthening of national competency, since national parliaments will have eight weeks in which to raise objections against proposed EU legislation.
6. The number of commissioners will be reduced from twenty-seven to fifteen by 2014.
7. A move toward closer cooperation in judicial and police matters, as well as social affairs, but with the chance for member states to opt out.
8. The extension of majority voting to asylum, immigration, as well as judicial and police cooperation in criminal matters.
9. The lifting of restrictions on the European Court of Justice to rule on cases with a JHA dimension.

Alas, as with the Maastricht Treaty, some member states secured opt-outs, thereby adding further asymmetry to what was once a uniform EU. The Charter of Fundamental Rights, for instance, would not be applicable to Poland and the UK, while Ireland, Denmark, and the UK secured opt-outs for asylum, visa, and immigration, with Britain deciding on a case-by-case basis whether to join EU initiatives in these fields.

It is fair to say that at least some provisions of the Lisbon Treaty will be implemented. Despite the treaty's rejection by the Irish public, certain institutional modifications can be taken on board without the need for a new treaty. Nonetheless, is it true that the EU has reached at least a momentary end point in its drive for ever more integration? One might want to glance at Lisbon's treaty provision of "enhanced cooperation." According to this clause, at least one-third of EU member states (i.e., in 2009, nine countries) may work together more closely on JHA issues, without needing the support of other member states as long as these are not affected by any such measures. The clause has the potential to add to an already asymmetric EU, with some member states wishing for more and others for less integration.

2

Enlargement

During the 1950s and 1960s the emerging European Union was only one of several al-
ternatives for fostering cooperation among European states. The European Free Trade
Association (EFTA) at one stage had more members than the European Union had.[1]
But when Britain first applied for membership to the European Economic Community
in 1961, it became clear that the EU was indeed highly attractive, especially because
the development of a unified market promised expanding trade relations. Over subse-
quent years, one European state after the other handed in its application, and we can
now safely claim that the EU has become the primary vehicle for organizing Europe.
But expanding the membership has also been attractive to existing member states.
Not only did enlargement offer more markets, it also increased stability and security
on the continent, and some member states, such as the UK and Denmark, welcomed
enlargement as a way to water down ambitions for greater political integration.

After a brief history of the successive enlargement rounds of the EU, this chapter
offers insights into why and how the EU has integrated new members, especially the
ambitious 2004 round that expanded the union in one sweep from fifteen to twenty-five
members. This is followed by a discussion of future enlargements and an analysis of
how the EU might be able to cope with an ever expanding membership. The key issues
surrounding enlargement are:

1. What explains the speed of enlargement?
2. How does the European Union enlarge?
3. What are the costs and benefits of enlargement for the current members?
4. What are the costs and benefits of enlargement for the accession states?

History of Enlargement

The first round of enlargement could have happened as early as 1961, had it not been for the then French president Charles de Gaulle. The French leader vigorously opposed Britain's membership application on the grounds that British interests in the Community were mainly in the field of trade and market access, with no firm commitments to other policies, most notably agriculture. Hence Britain's first application was turned down, as was the second in 1967. Twice de Gaulle put his foot down, declaring that the UK lacked a true European vocation. When George Pompidou succeeded de Gaulle in 1969, however, progress on the British application was swift. Battling against a skeptical public, which found both the successor to its empire—the Commonwealth—as well as close relations with America more appealing than membership in the EC, UK Prime Minister Edward Heath nonetheless managed to convince his ruling Conservative Party of the growing importance of European trade partners for British industry. He effectively used the argument that EU economies had continuously outperformed their British counterpart, which meant that the UK had fallen further and further behind the continent in terms of prosperity. As for Denmark and Ireland, their applications were always connected to that of the UK, since both countries had strong trade relations with Britain. With the first round of enlargement, then, the union changed in a number of ways: the special relationship between Britain and the United States gave the EU a stronger global link; the accession of Ireland provided for the inclusion of an economically backward state, where economic performance and development lagged far behind the union's average; and the acceptance of Denmark and the UK meant that the EU, for the first time, had to confront a higher degree of skepticism toward European integration, particularly political union, than had previously existed among the original six founding states.

The second enlargement, in 1981, involved Greece and repeated the Ireland experience almost a decade earlier in that Greece was another economically backward country joining the community to boost trade and the country's standard of living. In contrast to Ireland, however, the EU had to address the political dimension of this accession. After seven years of Junta rule (1967–1974), the European Council thought that a speedy integration of Greece would offer a much-needed buffer of popular support to a still tender democracy.

Political stabilization also played a role in the third enlargement in 1986. Both Spain and Portugal had only recently, in the mid 1970s, emerged from authoritarian rule.[2] A short-lived coup in Spain in 1982 highlighted the shaky foundations on which the two Iberian democracies were built. Up until that year, accession negotiations were cumbersome, as Italy and France were concerned about the perceived competition in agricultural produce such as wine, olives, and tomatoes, while other member states worried about the prospect of cheap labor moving to northern Europe and the size of the Spanish fishing fleet. In the end, however, the coup of 1982 reaffirmed the notion that membership in the European club offered a crucial degree of democratic stability, especially since Spain and Portugal were also members of NATO.

In contrast to the often acrimonious negotiations with the Iberian countries, the fourth round of 1995 posed no major problems. With the end of the Cold War, the three formerly neutral countries, Finland, Sweden, and Austria, lost their political rationale as buffers between East and West. Instead, the economic benefits of gaining access to a highly integrated market now dominated the agenda. In contrast to previous rounds, the gross domestic product (GDP) of the three newcomers was well above EU average. This naturally pleased poorer member states, as it posed no upcoming challenge to their status as main beneficiaries of the EU's cohesion funds. It was no surprise, therefore, that accession was speedily negotiated merely three years after the applications were submitted. Only minor difficulties arose over environmental damage in the Austrian Alps through increased truck traffic, and agricultural problems concerning Austrian hill farmers and North Scandinavian tundra farmers.[3]

With these four enlargement rounds the EU had turned into the world's largest market, with some 340 million consumers. Fifty years after the end of World War II, the Union was also the world's leading commercial power, attracting 20 percent of global imports and exports, excluding intra EU trade. However, EU institutions were designed for a union of six states, not fifteen; indeed, the nature of the EU had changed considerably. In particular, the Franco-German axis—long the driving force of European integration—became less prominent over the years. Although calls for further European integration still often originated in Berlin and Paris, with many more members and divergent sets of interests, agreements were not always as straightforward as the two old partners would have liked.

The European Union did not stop at fifteen, however. With the end of communism, nearly all former Soviet satellite states decided that their economic and political futures were linked to a closer integration within the European Union. Between March 1994 (Hungary) and January 1996 (Czech Republic) ten Central and Eastern European Countries (CEEC) submitted their applications to Brussels. The two noncommunist states of Cyprus and Malta had already done so in July 1990. Obviously, integrating such a large number of countries imposed severe challenges. First, the number of EU citizens would increase by 32 percent to 485 million. Second, the level of economic development in the CEEC was sharply below those of Western Europe. In fact, upon accession in 2004, the absolute GDP of the EU grew by only 8 percent. Although per capita income in Slovenia (the most prosperous application

Table 2.1. Chronology of Enlargement

Year	Membership Count	Countries
1951	original 6	West Germany, France, Italy, Belgium, Luxembourg, and the Netherlands
1973	9	UK, Ireland, and Denmark
1981	10	Greece
1986	12	Portugal and Spain
1995	15	Sweden, Finland, and Austria
2004	25	Malta, Cyprus, Estonia, Latvia, Lithuania, Poland, Hungary, Czech Republic, Slovakia, and Slovenia
2007	27	Bulgaria and Romania
beyond	35*	Croatia, Macedonia, Turkey, Albania, Bosnia-Herzegovina, Serbia, Montenegro, and Ukraine

* Membership could even rise to 36 countries once Kosovo gains full independence. Montenegro voted for independence from Serbia in May 2006 and, like its neighbors in the region, also decided to apply for EU membership.

country) was 74 percent of the EU average and in line with that of Portugal, incomes in Latvia were only 35 percent of the EU average.[4] In the run up to accession, the developmental needs of all the candidate countries were therefore significant and covered every conceivable economic, political, and administrative sector. The EU tried to address this challenge with a series of programs, including support for the modernization of agriculture, environmental and infrastructural programs, and twinning schemes (the secondment of civil servants from the EU-15 to the accession states) with public administrations from the EU-15. The programs were designed to bring the candidates to an acceptable level of development that would make them ready for membership.[5]

The EU itself was also trying to get ready for enlargement. The objective of the summit meeting in Nice in December 2000 was to provide institutional and policy reforms preparatory to the upcoming wave of accession. Nice produced some results, most notably the reweighing of votes in the Council of Ministers. However, a number of crucial items were not addressed and were postponed for another intergovernmental round of negotiations. These items included, first of all, an agreement on the size of the budget. Integrating poorer countries necessarily required the potential expansion of the Common Agricultural Policy and the Cohesion funds for a smooth extension of the Single Market and of EMU. Yet Commission proposals to reform the budget were largely put on hold by the member states. The financial perspective covering the years 2000 to 2006 was left untouched, and the enlargement of 2004 was financed without additional budget contributions from the existing member states.

Second, a pressing problem demanding closer attention was agriculture, especially in countries with large rural populations such as in Poland. The Commission's proposals were approved by the member states as late as December 2002.[6]

Further, the EU's cohesion policy needed to be completely overhauled to cope with so many countries where economic development still lagged far behind that of Western Europe. But again the EU decided to stick to existing spending plans, with an overhaul of cohesion promised for the next financial perspective covering the years 2007 to 2013.

By the end of 2002, ten countries had successfully completed their negotiations, and the final seal of approval for integrating the new member states was given by the Copenhagen summit in December of that year. In May 2004 the union expanded to twenty-five states. All applicants were included except Romania and Bulgaria; the Commission deemed that the administrative capacities of the two Balkan countries was too weak, particularly their judicial systems, and gave them 2007 as a later date for accession.

Analyzing Enlargement: Key Principles

The EU follows four main principles in pursuing its objectives for enlargement and for imposing requirements on the candidate countries. The first principle is that the EU insists on the full acceptance of the acquis communautaire. The acquis refers to the total set of rights and obligations attached to the European Union that emerged out of the EU's legislative processes. Hence, the acquis consists of all treaties, EU legislation, and case law as developed by the European Court of Justice that were passed since the Treaty of Paris in 1951. It also includes every policy, including EMU, since opt-outs are not granted to new member states. This massive set of laws, rules, and regulations, totaling some ninety thousand pages in the English version, must be integrated into a candidate's national law before membership is granted. Because future members have to satisfy this requirement to qualify for admission, negotiations to join the EU have become increasingly difficult, complex, and time-consuming— especially in view of the ever growing acquis—both for the countries holding the Presidency, which conducts the negotiations, and for the applicant countries.

The second principle is that the EU tends to address diversity by creating new policy instruments. Each round of enlargement showed that the economic structures of the new member states did not fit existing patterns within the EU of expenditures and incomes. The accession of the UK in 1973, for instance, was complicated by the country's large quantities of cheaper food imported from Commonwealth countries, which clashed with the Common Agricultural Policy (CAP). In return for Britain's acceptance of the CAP, the EU agreed to establish a Regional Development Fund (ERDF) to support regions with lower economic output and productivity. So, instead of making structural adjustments to key polices such as the CAP, the EU preferred to keep those policies relatively untouched and instead established new policies that offset detrimental consequences.

As a third principle, the EU integrates new member states with few adjustments to its institutions but promises to review the institutional operations in the future.

Table 2.2. Principles of Enlargement

1. Full acceptance of the acquis communautaire
2. Addressing diversity through new policies
3. Integration through limited institutional adaptation
4. Preferring groups of states over individual applicants (exception: Greece, 1981).

Source: C. Preston, "Obstacles to EU Enlargement: The Classical Community Method and the Prospects for a Wider Europe," *Journal of Common Market Studies* 33, no. 3 (1995): 451–463.

The years have seen only slow progress in institutional adaptations as new members joined the Commission, the European Parliament, and the Council of Ministers. No institutional innovations have occurred in parallel with enlargement. In marked contrast, the summit meeting in Nice in December 2000 represented a change in direction. Nice reached an agreement on far-reaching institutional reforms, since a union of twenty-five members by 2004 and twenty-seven members by 2007 would make effective governance under the old system very difficult. In the end, the EU set new limits to the size of the European Parliament (capped at 732) and the Commission (a maximum of 27 commissioners), and also changed the voting procedure in the Council of Ministers.

The EU's fourth principle is its preference to negotiate with groups of states that already have close relations with one another. This principle is a coherent theme throughout all EU enlargement processes, with the notable exception of Greece in 1981. For example, in 1973, prior to joining the EU, the UK and Ireland, as well as the UK and Denmark, had already established strong trade links. Moreover, the EU did not attempt to decouple the relatively straightforward applications of Denmark and Ireland from the complicated British negotiations, where the terms for British entry (CAP and the budget) took years to be finalized.[7]

How Does the EU Enlarge?

At a summit meeting of the European Council in Copenhagen in 1993, the EU established a blueprint for how future accessions should be managed. The so-called Copenhagen criteria concentrated especially on a country's democratic institutions that ought to guarantee key liberal democratic principles promoted by the EU.[8] Every new member state also has to make the necessary economic adjustments in order to cope with the competitive pressures of the Single Market. A new administrative criterion was developed to ensure the presence of institutional capacities that guaranteed the continual implementation of EU law. This criterion focuses on the candidate's public administration, testing whether the bureaucracy, from ministries to law enforcement agencies and to courts, would be able to fulfill their functions against an ever increasing stream of legislation issuing from Brussels. In light of the Maastricht Treaty and its widespread reforms (which had entered into

Table 2.3. The Copenhagen Criteria for Enlargement

1. Political Criterion	Institutional guarantee of democracy, human rights, the rule of law, and respect for and protection of minorities
2. Economic Criterion	A functioning market economy, with the capacity to cope with competitive pressure and market forces
3. Administrative Criterion	Assuming the obligations of membership (i.e., adhering to the acquis communautaire)

force a few months earlier), the Copenhagen criteria also required that the capacity to absorb new member states should not jeopardize the momentum of European integration.

When a country applies for membership, the Commission's responsibility is to assess a candidate's suitability for joining the union. The Commission therefore starts an intense dialogue that focuses initially on the political criteria. The entire acquis is then subdivided into negotiation chapters, which, in the case of the 2004 enlargement, totaled thirty-one. For instance, there were separate chapters on agriculture, the environment, and transport. The EU country holding the Presidency chairs the negotiations, with the help of the Commission, and each chapter is addressed individually. Once negotiations reach a satisfactory conclusion, the Commission writes a report to the European Parliament and the European Council; both bodies must then agree to the applicant's membership, in Parliament with an absolute majority and in the Council by unanimity.

Who's Next? Future Enlargements

The European Union continues to be highly attractive for its neighbors and, beyond the 2004 and 2007 enlargement, additional countries are knocking on the door in Brussels. As of 2008, Turkey, Croatia, and Macedonia have the status of candidates. and Serbia, Montenegro, Albania, and Bosnia and Herzegovina have also expressed interest in joining. After the 2004 regime change in the Ukraine, that country might also consider a future application. Hence the total membership of the EU could rise significantly (see Table 2.1). A number of obstacles must be overcome as the EU considers the possibility of admitting Croatia, Turkey, Macedonia, and several West Balkan states.

Croatia signed a so-called Stabilization and Association Agreement (SAA) with the EU in October 2001. In February 2003 the country applied for membership; this objective was endorsed by the European Commission, and in June 2004 candidate status was granted when the European Council decided that the accession process should be launched. The start of negotiations was scheduled for March 2005 but was delayed by the controversy surrounding the suspected war criminal Ante Gotovina, who, as an army general, gained the status of a national hero in the 1995 war between

Croatia and Serbia. From the outset, the EU expected that all suspected war criminals would be surrendered to the International Criminal Tribunal for the Former Yugoslavia in the Dutch capital of The Hague. The capture of Gotovina in December 2005, therefore, paved the way for accession negotiations to start in earnest.

Turkey arguably represents the EU's biggest challenge. Much debate has already occurred over whether the union should integrate a country with a predominantly Muslim population, especially as public opinion in France and Germany is fiercely divided over this issue. Moreover, Turkey's population of 70 million would make it the EU's second most populous member state with significant voting powers in the Council of Ministers. Given Turkey's low prosperity levels—around 25 percent of the average EU level and similar to that of Bulgaria and Romania—the possibility of considerable migratory movements to northern and western Europe was also causing concern in some member states. For these reasons, Turkey's application has repeatedly been put on hold, although it had applied for membership as early as 1987.

In November 2002, however, with the election of Prime Minister Recep Tayyip Erdogan, Turkey's application was taken up again. Two years later the Commission issued a positive report confirming that the country met the political criteria and suggested that accession negotiations should commence in the fall of 2005. Nonetheless, the Commission delivered a number of warning shots, stressing that "accession cannot take place before 2014, and that it must be thoroughly prepared to allow for smooth integration and to avoid endangering the achievements of over fifty years of European integration." More specifically, the Commission demanded an annual review of the progress of political reforms in Turkey and would recommend suspending negotiations if any principles of the political criteria were seriously and persistently breached.

Relations between the EU and Turkey were further strained by the continuous controversy over Cyprus. Ankara has refused to give diplomatic recognition to the Republic of Cyprus, though it is an EU member, and has closed off all its ports and airports to goods and people from that part of the island.[9] EU member states argued, however, that progress in Turkey's path toward Europe could only be achieved if the Turkish government reversed its position. In fact, the EU, lead by the Finnish Presidency, even threatened to suspend negotiations should Ankara refuse to give in. In the end, a last-minute compromise was reached at the EU summit in December 2006, with Turkey opening at least one port to the Greek-Cypriot lead Republic. Therefore, in view of Turkey's size, economic backwardness, and the painstaking and time-consuming efforts to reform its political system, an accession date of 2014, which has been suggested, seems rather optimistic.

It is very possible that Macedonia will join the EU before Turkey does. As with Croatia, the country signed an SAA with the EU in April 2001, and the proper application for membership followed in March 2004. Although the political situation remains relatively stable, paramount to the EU is a successful integration of the sizable ethnic minority of Albanians. In a 2006 report, the Commission also listed such challenges as corruption, as well as needed reforms of the police and judiciary. This assessment, however, represented a marked improvement from the 2005 report, which noted "serious weaknesses in the functioning of the economy, business climate, competitiveness and enforcement of property rights," as well as weak foreign direct investment. In that year the Commission proposed that accession negotiations with Macedonia ought to begin, and in December 2005 the European Council agreed. Nonetheless, given the multitude of problems with the application, the Commission so far has refrained from even approximating the date when the country might be able to join.

The Western Balkans—Albania, Bosnia and Herzegovina, Serbia,[10] and Montenegro[11]—are included in the framework of the Stabilization and Association Process (SAP)[12] with the purpose of preparing them for future membership. As with the candidates for the 2004 and 2007 enlargements, the Copenhagen criteria formed the basis of any negotiations. Financial assistance was given as part of a program called the Community Assistance for Reconstruction, Development, and Stabilization (CARDS), for which the EU had earmarked five billion Euro for the period from 2000 to 2006. CARDS was mainly used for infrastructure, institution building, and matters related to justice and home affairs.

Since September 2000 the EU has granted the countries of the region wide-ranging free access to the union's market for almost all goods, with the aim of boosting economic development. Also, regarding regional cooperation, the Commission reported positively on a number of agreements that were concluded on the return of refugees, border crossings, visa regimes, the fight against terrorism, and organized crime. In its frequent assessments, however, the Commission listed a number of political-structural problems that needed to be rectified in order for a serious accession process to begin. The problems include the functioning of government institutions; reform of the educational systems, public administration, and judicial systems; corruption; respect for human and minority rights; gender equality; the return of refugees; and media legislation.

Bosnia and Herzegovina, as well as Serbia, recently managed to fulfill the required conditions for "upgrading their status" in the form of signing an SAA, which necessitated meeting the specific criteria of the SAP, including complete cooperation with the International Criminal Tribunal for the Former Yugoslavia (ICTY), respect for minority rights, opportunities for displaced persons and refugees to return home, and a clear commitment to regional cooperation. In Serbia's case, the Commission stated in April 2005 that progress on reform remained fragile, but it acknowledged that the country had significantly improved its economic and political capacities and its ability to negotiate and implement an SAA. Hence the Commission recommended to the European Council the opening of negotiations. On the other hand, Enlargement Commissioner Olli Rehn continued to remind Belgrade that Serbia had little chance of formalizing closer links with the EU as long as two suspected war criminals—General Ratko Mladić and Radovan Karadžić—remain at large.[13] As a result, in May 2006, the EU suspended negotiations with Serbia on the grounds that both men were still at large. Negotiations resumed in June 2007 after the country elected a new government, and the SAA was signed in April 2008.

Discussions between the EU and Bosnia and Herzegovina were based on the Commission's Feasibility Study of March 2003 in which Brussels listed sixteen priorities, including political dialogue and economic, police, judiciary, and other reforms, that should be addressed before the EU would agree to closer contractual relations. By 2005, progress was made on meeting these objectives and the European Council began SAA negotiations in November of that year, which concluded in December 2007.

Regarding Albania, negotiations for an SAA started in February 2003. In a 2005 Progress Report, the Commission noted improvements in a number of areas but called for better results in fighting organized crime and corruption, enhanced media freedom, further electoral reform, and swifter property restitution. Nonetheless, the report concluded that Albania's progress in reforms had paved the way for the finalization of SAA negotiations, which concluded in 2006.[14]

The objective of the EU with regard to the Western Balkans seems straightforward. Membership cannot be denied to these countries as long as they meet strict criteria—not only the enlargement criteria as applied in 2004 but also the requirement for regional, cross-border cooperation as a vehicle for turning former enemies into partners. Given that these countries remain economically behind Western European levels, it seems safe to say that they still have a mountain to climb before serious accession negotiations can start.

PART TWO

INSTITUTIONS

Institutional relations within the EU represent a carefully struck balance between intergovernmental forces and supranational institutions. This chapter analyzes the EU's six main institutions—the European Commission, the Council of Ministers, the Presidency, the European Council, the European Parliament, and the European Court of Justice—along with the institutional checks and balance. The institutional analysis focuses on five key issues:

1. The legislative, executive, and judiciary powers of the institutions
2. The reasons why member states have delegated powers in certain areas to supranational institutions but maintained sovereignty in other intergovernmental institutions
3. The criticism that some institutions are facing in relation to the perceived democratic deficit and lack of transparency
4. The balance of power between the institutions
5. The ways in which member states can control and influence policy-making processes in Brussels

3

The European Commission

Organization

The European Commission is led by the Commission President, with the assistance of twenty-six commissioners, the equivalent of "ministers" at the national level.[1] Just as with any national administration, these politicians have staffs made up of many civil servants, the so-called Eurocrats. Whereas the commissioners usually come and go at five-year intervals, the Eurocrats have longer-term appointments, with many staff members of the Commission's civil service spending a large portion of their professional lives in Brussels. The organization of the Commission differs from national governments in a number of ways, reflecting the dual nature of the EU as both an intergovernmental union of states and a supranational union of European citizens.

First, the election of the Commission President is less straightforward than national elections of presidents or prime ministers, who receive their political legitimacy simply through elections. In the EU, all twenty-seven heads of government must agree on one candidate.[2]

Second, whereas presidents and prime ministers appoint their team of ministers and assign them particular responsibilities, such as foreign affairs, defense, or

Table 3.1. The European Commission, 2004–2009

Commission President: Jose Manuel Barroso, Portugal	
Commissioners	Portfolio
Günter Verheugen, Germany	Enterprise and Industry
Charlie McGreevy, Ireland	Internal Market
Neelie Kroes, Netherlands	Competition
Jaques Barrot, France	Transport
Franco Frattini, Italy	Justice
Peter Mandelson, UK	Trade
Margot Wallström, Sweden	Institutional Relations
Siim Kallas, Estonia	Administration, Audit, and Anti-Fraud
Olli Rehn, Finland	Enlargement
Danuta Hübner, Poland	Regional Policy
Dalia Grybauskaite, Lithuania	Financial Programming
Joaquin Almunia, Spain	Monetary Affairs
Benita Ferrero-Waldner, Austria	External Relations
Mariann Fischer Boel, Denmark	Agriculture
Joe Borg, Malta	Fisheries and Maritime
Laszlo Kovacs, Hungary	Taxation and Customs
Stavros Dimas, Greece	Environment
Markos Kyprianou, Cyprus	Health and Consumer
Vladimir Spidla, Czech Republic	Employment and Social Affairs
Louis Michel, Belgium	Humanitarian Aid
Janez Potocnik, Slovenia	Science and Research
Viviane Reding, Luxembourg	Information Society/Media
Jan Figel, Slovakia	Education and Culture
Andris Piebalgs, Latvia	Energy
Meglena Kuneva, Bulgaria*	Consumer Protection
Leonard Orban, Romania*	Multilinguism

*Joined the Commission in 2007.

finance, the individual commissioners are appointed by the national governments, and the governments negotiate with one another over which ministerial responsibilities their candidates will have. Although this should be done in collaboration with the Commission President, some member states often insist on certain portfolios and the Commission President has little say in the matter.[3] Not surprisingly, the larger countries often secure more attractive and influential portfolios, and the Commission President then has to balance and juggle portfolios and candidates to form a coherent administration.

The choice of commissioners, therefore, is crucial for the course of European integration. Knowledgeable and motivated commissioners obviously contribute more to the European cause than candidates who might be past their political prime.[4]

Naturally the choice of candidates deeply impacts the Commission President's performance. Imagine the president of the United States having to work with secretaries of state that are appointed by the representatives of the fifty states, who then even dictate to the president which secretary of state will manage which portfolio.

Despite these restrictions imposed on the Commission President, the fact is that the political influence of this post depends largely on the president's personal characteristics and policy ideals.[5] All twenty-seven commissioners (the College of Commissioners) usually meet once a week to discuss legislative proposals. When voting on whether to proceed with a legislative initiative, a simple majority decides the issue with the Commission President exercising the deciding vote in case of a tie.

Despite the prominent scapegoating in Western Europe of a Brussels bureaucracy of vast proportions, only some twenty-four thousand civil servants work for the Commission. The EU bureaucracy is composed of twenty-six so-called Directorate Generals (DGs) and nine services,[6] which are the organizational equivalents of government ministries in national administrations, and they fulfill many of the same functions as ministerial departments: policy development, preparation of legislation, monitoring of legislative implementation, and advice and support for the political executive.

Neither the number nor the responsibilities of the DGs correspond exactly to the number of commissioner portfolios, and, indeed, commissioners may have more than one DG at their disposal. Alternatively, a DG may be responsible for the portfolios of more than one commissioner. Conversely, a commissioner might not have a DG at all, which is somewhat similar to the position of a minister without a portfolio in parliamentary governments.

Every commissioner has a supporting cabinet, reflecting a strong French tradition in the organization of EU administration. Most cabinets have seven members, career Eurocrats or political appointees, whom the commissioner brings to Brussels. Their job is to facilitate the work of the commissioner, such as acting as liaison with other commissioners and between different DGs, or organizing and sometimes chairing committee meetings. A good cabinet undoubtedly can boost a commissioner's standing, whereas a bad cabinet can impair a commissioner's influence on the Brussels administration. It is no coincidence that the most effective commissioners have the best staffed and best organized cabinets.

The Commission recruits its personnel through an extremely competitive, EU-wide selection process that includes aptitude and language proficiency tests, written examinations, and interviews. From the beginning of their careers, the Commission civil servants enter a world of unofficial but nonetheless finely balanced national quotas. The EU administration needs to reflect the population size and distribution of each member states. Hence promotions through the ranks are subject to an unofficial allocation of positions to each member state at every step of a civil servant's career ladder. Promotions to senior positions are highly political, not only because there are fewer jobs available compared to the number of lower positions,

Table 3.2. Directorates General and Services of the European Commission, 2004–2009

Policies	External Relations
Agriculture and Rural Development	Development
Competition	Enlargement
Economic and Financial Affairs	EuropeAid—Cooperation Office
Education and Culture	External Relations
Employment, Social Affairs, and Equal Opportunities	Humanitarian Aid Office—ECHO
Enterprise and Industry	Trade
Environment	
Fisheries and Maritime Affairs	**General Services:**
Health and Consumer Protection	European Anti Fraud Office
Information Society and Media	Eurostat
Internal Market and Services	Press and Communications
Joint Research Center	Publications Office
Justice, Freedom and Security	Secretariat General
Regional Policy	
Research	**Internal Services**
Taxation and Customs Union	Budget
Transport and Energy	Group of Policy Advisers
	Informatics
	Infrastructures and Logistics
	Internal Audit Service
	Interpretation
	Legal Service
	Personnel and Administration
	Translation

but national civil servants who are brought in from outside, such as cabinet members, further reduce the availability of senior jobs. The difficulty of progressing to senior jobs causes much frustration and resentment, especially as the obsession with national quotas means that a Eurocrat's professional competence and merit is not necessarily reflected in the level of his or her post.[7]

Powers and Responsibilities

The Commission plays six key roles: proposing legislation, implementing EU policies, managing the budget, conducting external relations, policing EU laws, and pointing the way forward.

1. *Proposing legislation.* Typically, in democratic systems, a number of political actors can propose legislation. In the EU, however, only the Commission can both propose legislation and initiate the process of determining whether the proposal will become law. Other institutions, such as the European Council or the European

Table 3.3. Powers of the European Commission

Legislative Powers:
    Proposing legislation
Executive Powers:
    Implementing EU policies
    Managing the Budget
    Conducting External Relations
    Policing EU law
    Pointing the way forward

Parliament, may ask the Commission to initiate legislation, but proposals predominately originate within the Commission. Most of the Commission's proposals have a clear legal base in the treaties. The Single European Act, for instance, elevated the subject of the environment to the European level, and from then on the Commission could propose legislation in this field. Other legislative proposals can flow from legislation already adopted—a legislative spillover to complete a particular policy or program, and others could originate in a particular court ruling by the European Court of Justice.

Within the Commission, proposals can follow different paths. The Commission President, an individual commissioner, the head of a DG, or even a section director can ask staff to prepare proposals. Even ambitious junior Eurocrats may bombard their superiors with ideas. On the other hand, proposals can also come about in response to a suggestion by a member state or an interest group. Annual legislative consultations also occur with other EU institutions, such as the European Parliament and the Council of Ministers, where the general agenda and priorities for the upcoming year are debated. Whatever the origin of a legislative proposal, it has to work its way through the Commission's internal committees that coordinate various parts of the Commission, as well as external committees where outside experts or national civil servants are consulted.

2. *Implementing EU policies.* More prominent than its role in legislation is the Commission's position as the executive authority of the EU. Whereas national governments have vast human resources to implement or enforce legislation, for example, police forces, customs officials, and tax authorities, the Commission has no such services but must rely on national authorities to assist in this area. National veterinary services, for instance, monitor EU regulations governing the health of livestock, and national customs officials check baggage at airports when travelers enter the geographical space of the European common market. Because the Commission depends entirely on this kind of support, it concentrates its executive powers on passing concrete rules and regulations that turn legislation into practice. The Commission issues around five thousand directives, regulations, and decisions annually, mainly on technical aspects of EU policies. Based on this authority, the

Commission does have a great impact on the daily lives of Europeans by specifying such matters as product guidelines, environmental standards, and health and safety features.[8] The Commission's implementation power is also illustrated by its role in enlargement. Based on legal criteria that candidate countries must satisfy in order to qualify, the Commission monitors the progress of each accession state until the candidate has reached the required EU norms. The Commission then issues a final report that the member states and the European Parliament use to decide whether to approve an application.

3. *Managing the budget.* The EU budget is relatively small, comprising only 1 percent of the EU's GNP,[9] and each year the Commission submits a draft budget to the member states and the European Parliament. The draft serves as a material basis for the EU's political, economic, and social objectives, one of which is to distribute financial support to members in need of help, such as farmers or economically backward regions. Technically the Commission manages the budget, yet the member states make the political decisions on how it should be spend.

4. *Conducting external relations.* The Commission maintains some one hundred offices and delegations across the globe. Although the heads of these delegations have the diplomatic status of ambassadors, this does not mean that the EU is comparable to a foreign service. The Common Foreign and Security Policy is under the exclusive authority of member states, whereas the Commission's external relations mainly concern trade and technical issues. Still, in the area of international trade, the Commission has proven to be a highly capable player. At the World Trade Organization (WTO), it is the Commission that negotiates on behalf of all EU member states.[10] Although association and accession agreements are negotiated by the country holding the Presidency of the EU and approved by the member states and the European Parliament, the Commission is heavily involved because it assesses the progress in meeting entrance criteria of an accession country and suggests to the member states how to proceed with a particular candidate.

5. *Policing EU laws.* The Commission is sometimes referred to as the "guardian of the treaties," a rather grand description of its powers in this field. Still, under Article 169 of the Treaty of Rome, the Commission has the authority to bring member states before the Court of Justice for alleged non-fulfillment of a treaty obligation. Usually, however, member states fulfill their treaty commitments; otherwise, the EU would simply collapse. Although countries frequently fail to comply, particularly in the area of the Single Market, it is often the result of a genuine misunderstanding or misinterpretation of Commission rules, or of delays in translating EU legislation into national law. If the Commission takes a member state to the European Court of Justice in Luxembourg, the case results in a highly publicized and potentially embarrassing political affair. The member states and the Commission, therefore, are generally reluctant to pursue cases all the way to the ECJ, as the negative publicity it generates is detrimental to both the Commission and the member state involved. Parties try to resolve most disputes at an early stage.

6. *Pointing the way forward.* This considerable power is best exemplified by the former Commission president Jacques Delors, who declared, in 1987, that the Commission has a unique obligation to point the way to the goal ahead. He explained that the Commission alone cannot achieve much, but it can generate ideas. Its main weapon is conviction. There are numerous examples, the most prominent, perhaps, is the Single Market. Based on the prospect of falling behind the U.S. and Japan, the member states undoubtedly were eager to complete the common market by the early 1990s, but it was the Commission that put the package together after mapping out a strategy on how to succeed. In contrast, the EU stagnates when the Commission and its president are unable to lead. The tenures of Jacques Santer (1994–1999) and Romano Prodi (1999–2004) fall into this category.

4

The European Council

Organization

The European Council, commonly termed the "Summit," is made up of the political leaders of the member states, such as prime ministers, as well as the president of the European Commission. Foreign ministers also attend, but they are not considered members. The Summit usually meets four times a year.[1]

The European Council was not mentioned in the Treaty of Rome and therefore was not part of the original institutional setup. But at the Paris summit in 1974, French President Valerie Giscard d'Estaing convinced his fellow heads of government that the Union needed a regular and high-profile organization that would allow national leaders to more aggressively shape the direction and speed of European integration. The institutional framework of the European Community was ill-equipped for increased cooperation at the highest level, and it could not offer the kind of distinct authority and leadership that Giscard believed only the heads of government could provide. Nearly two decades later, the Maastricht Treaty acknowledged the Summit's function as "providing the Union with the necessary impetus for its development and shall define the general guidelines thereof." Hence the primary function of the European Council can be described as that of a central political leadership which sets objectives, particularly for the long-term development of the EU.

Table 4.1. The European Council

- Comprised of national heads of government, and the President and Vice President of the European Commission
- Meets about four times a year
- Provides overall direction to the EU

Today, more than ever, the primary function of the European Council is to give strategic direction to the EU by going beyond the boundaries of national interests and viewing the union as an organic whole. The Summit also has the distinct advantage of acquainting political leaders with one another and introducing new heads of government into this exclusive, but often rather informal, European club. Because media coverage of the EU has soared over recent years, clever politicians have frequently used this publicity for public relations exercises that often serve domestic political purposes. This often undermined Giscard's initial intention of providing an informal forum where national leaders could debate and exchange ideas freely without intense media scrutiny.

Working Mechanisms

1. *Preparing meetings.* The task of preparing Summit meetings is largely the responsibility of the member state holding the EU Presidency. The extent of a member state's initiative is, of course, subject to the agenda that a country wants to achieve during its Presidency. Some countries like to retain a low profile, merely circulating documents, information, and organizational matters. Most often, however, member states see the Presidency as a chance to shape the agenda of the EU and to seek a very active and public role. Hence national officials of the country holding the Presidency usually initiate meetings months before the start of a summit, with other national officials, the secretariat of the Council of Ministers, and the Commission. These preparatory meetings are usually concluded some ten days prior to a summit, when the foreign ministers meet to finalize the agenda.

2. *Issues discussed.* Some items are so important that they are always on the agenda. These usually include discussion of the general economic situation, the Single Market, and, more recently, EMU and enlargement. The Commission also might focus on an issue in which it is particularly interested, such as debating about the reorganization of the budget or institutional reforms. Often the Presidency wants to pursue a particular agenda.[2] Sometimes discussions will resume on items that were not successfully concluded within the Council of Ministers or on other business remaining from previous summits. Finally, special attention may be given to international circumstances such as the war in Iraq or the war on terrorism in the aftermath of the bombings in Madrid and London.[3]

3. *How the Summit actually works.* On the first day of the Summit, heads of governments, their ministers, and Commission officials meet for extensive talks.

Lunch is usually a lengthy affair (as it allows for informal debates in a relaxed atmosphere) and is followed by more rounds of discussion. What happens after dinner depends on the progress that was made over the course of the day. Sometimes heads of government retire to fireside chats, conducive for informal consultations. Other times, prime ministers have to forfeit brandy and a log fire and hammer out the final wording of agreements. Once these agreements are concluded, the Presidency staff and the Council of Ministers work feverishly throughout the night to prepare the draft conclusions that will be discussed by the heads of government on the morning of the second day. The summit often ends on the afternoon of the second day with a final statement and press conference.[4] The statement is usually agreed upon unanimously.[5]

Functions

1. *Setting the pace of integration.* The European Council informs the Commission of member states' preferences for the future direction of the European project, including new policies and institutional reforms. This is a high-profile event that the Commission cannot ignore, for it is the Commission's responsibility to turn the Summit's objectives into concrete legislative proposals. The Summit, therefore, might be referred to as an individual legislator.

2. *Providing an important arena for major policy initiatives.* An example of this function is the summit in Maastricht in 1991, which centered on the transition from the European Community to the EU with a Common Foreign and Security Policy (CFSP) and EMU, as well as developments in justice and home affairs. These extremely sensitive issues were hotly debated at this summit, and diverging opinions over the scope and practical consequences of these policies continue to determine the debate over the precise nature of the EU.

3. *Resolving problems.* Attempts are made to resolve potential disagreements in person-to-person discussions that offer the opportunity to broker deals and reach compromises. The European Council does not deal exclusively in one policy area, as does the Council of Ministers. It is therefore a very useful venue for deal making between member states where different policy areas are affected. The European Council proved to be a superb vehicle for resolving problems efficiently.

4. *Decision making.* The Summit also functions as a decision maker. Treaty amendments, new policies, and reforms are agreed upon in a unanimous fashion, and these decisions then have to be taken further by the European Commission (for Pillar I), as well as the Council of Ministers (for Pillars II and III).

5. *International player.* Exercising its responsibilities in the sphere of external relations, the Summit has, for example, imposed trade sanctions against apartheid South Africa, a weapons embargo against China, and, more recently, trade sanctions against Milosevic's Yugoslavia.

Table 4.2. Functions of The European Council

1. Sets the pace of integration
2. Initiates major policies
3. Resolves problems
4. Makes decisions
5. Serves as international player

Institutional Relations

In retrospect, without these top-level meetings, the EU would not have been able to survive the Eurosclerosis of the 1970s, and certainly would not have launched the Single Market program in the 1980s. The Summit, therefore, is far more than a glorified high-profile public relations exercise and, arguably, has been the most influential institution in the processes of European integration. At the same time, it is the epitome of intergovernmentalism in the Union; it is a thorn in the eye of passionate European federalists, since it upholds the national sovereignty of member states by sidelining supranational European institutions such as the Parliament (which is not involved in the Summit's agenda-setting or decision-making processes) or the Commission (which is only invited to participate in Summit proceedings).

The responsibility of the Commission to initiate policies is undoubtedly curtailed to some extent by the Summit, which decides on the direction of policies that have far-reaching effects. But depending on the status of its president, the Commission might achieve some balance by playing an active role. Although some decisions are now reached by the Summit and not in the meetings of the Council of Ministers, the hierarchies of these two institutions are not necessarily competitive, as both represent national interests. Indeed, there should be coherence between the policies pursued by heads of state at the Summit and their ministers in the Council of Ministers.

More important, in any case, is the position of the European Parliament, which is completely excluded from the Summit, apart from the opening address which is delivered by the Parliament's president. This, of course, is a big blow to federalists and, some might argue, to the democratic legitimacy of the EU.

5

The Council of Ministers

Organization

The Council of Ministers is a unique political body, having no equivalent in the democratic world.[1] It epitomizes the special nature of the European Union as an international organization that balances supranational tendencies but also has to safeguard and represent national interests. Its main objective is to set the EU's medium-term policy goals. It also approves the budget and legislation that were proposed by the European Commission (a function which it shares with the European Parliament). Finally, the Council of Ministers also holds certain executive powers in Pillar II (Common Foreign and Security Policy) and in Pillar III (Justice and Home Affairs).

The Council carries out its operations through several sub-councils with different responsibilities (see Table 5.1). Examples are the Environment Council, where all twenty-seven national environment ministers meet, and the General Affairs Council, which brings together the national foreign ministers. The number of Council meetings depends on the scope and intensity of a particular legislative program. Some sub-councils meet monthly, such as the Economic and Financial Affairs Council (ECOFIN), the Agriculture Council, and the General Affairs Council, whereas others, like the Transport Council, meet less frequently.

Table 5.1. Configuration of the Council of Ministers

- General Affairs and External Relations
- Economic and Financial Affairs
- Justice and Home Affairs
- Employment, Social Policy, Health, and Consumer Affairs
- Competitiveness
- Transport, Telecommunications, and Energy
- Agriculture and Fisheries
- Environment
- Education, Youth, and Culture

These sporadic meetings are insufficient for effective politics, and so as early as 1958 the Committee of Permanent Representatives, or Coreper,[2] was created to meet at least once weekly to provide support. The Coreper staff consists of junior and senior civil servants, usually the member states' ambassadors and deputy ambassadors to the EU, who prepare the agenda of the Council of Ministers and decide which sub-councils should consider a given issue. Coreper also arranges some two hundred working groups of national officials. These groups discuss technical aspects of legislative proposals coming from the Commission and requiring special knowledge and expertise. The Council's political machine, then, operates on three levels: proposals from the Commission are scrutinized in the working groups; the evaluations are examined by Coreper; and Coreper then prepares the material for final decisions in the sub-councils.

The Process of Decision Making

How decisions are made depends on provisions elaborated in the treaties outlining whether legislative proposals are agreed upon by unanimity or by qualified majority voting (QMV). A rough guideline is that issues involving vital national interests require unanimous support, whereas the others require only a QMV. Issues such as foreign and security policy, taxes, social policies, or budgetary matters are still decided by unanimity.

In QMV, every member state has a certain number of votes proportional to its population. The bigger states such as France, Germany, the UK, and Italy have twenty-seven votes, and smaller countries like Malta have only three. Legislation is then approved by the Council of Ministers under three conditions:[3]

1. A majority of states must approve the legislation
2. The majority is defined as representing at least 62 percent of the EU population
3. The majority must have at least 72.3 percent of votes in the Council of Ministers, which, from 2007 on, is 250 out of 345 total votes

Table 5.2. Qualified Majority Voting in the Council of Ministers

Conditions for Passing Legislation
- Approval by majority of member states
- Must represent at least 62 percent of the EU population
- Must represent at least 72.3 percent of votes (as of 2007: 250 out of 345 votes)

EU-15		Accession Countries Post 2004	
Country	Votes	Country	Votes
France	29	Poland	27
Germany	29	Romania*	14
Italy	29	Czech Republic	12
UK	29	Hungary	12
Spain	27	Bulgaria*	10
Netherlands	13	Lithuania	7
Belgium	12	Slovakia	7
Greece	12	Cyprus	4
Portugal	12	Estonia	4
Austria	10	Latvia	4
Sweden	10	Slovenia	4
Denmark	7	Malta	3
Ireland	7		
Finland	7		
Luxembourg	4		

*Joined the EU in 2007.

The system is complex and, perhaps, difficult for outsiders to comprehend, and it certainly runs counter to such vital democratic principles as transparency and equity. Hence the failed constitution of 2005 proposed a much easier version. Every country simply gets one vote. Legislation would then be passed if approved by 55 percent of the member states representing 65 percent of the EU population. The Reform Treaty that was negotiated in June 2007 reiterated this double majority principle; depending on ratification the cumbersome Nice formula might finally be replaced but not until 2014.

Powers

The Council has legislative and executive powers. Regarding legislation, at the start of the European Community the Council of Ministers enjoyed sole decision-making power. Since then, in an attempt to strengthen the democratic legitimacy of the integration process, member states have increasingly shared some of its legislative powers with the European Parliament. Shared power is seen, in particular, with association and accession treaties but also with standard EU legislation that is now

Table 5.3. Powers of the Council of Ministers

- Approves legislation emanating from the Commission (together with the European Parliament)
- Approves the Commission's Budget proposal (together with the European Parliament)
- Has sole executive power in Common Foreign and Security Policy and in Justice and Home Affairs

---

enacted within the triangle of the Commission, Parliament and the Council of Ministers.

One of the Council's executive powers is the approval of the EU budget. Although this responsibility is shared with the European Parliament, it is still fundamentally important, as the Council can influence spending priorities that directly affect the lives of EU citizens.

Another Council function is to set policy objectives, which is done by delegating the powers of implementing policy to the Commission. The Commission, with its large bureaucracy and specialized departments, is better equipped than the Council to tackle a variety of executive functions, especially in implementing economic polices in agriculture, the internal market, and the environment, as well as monitoring their implementation by member states. The Commission also has the advantage that, unlike the member states' ministers on the Council, it does not have to cope with domestic pressures.

Meanwhile, the Council exercises executive powers completely on its own in the fields of Common Foreign and Security Policy and partly in the field of Justice and Home Affairs, because, in these areas, the right to initiate policies remains with the member states. Politically sensitive executive powers and the vital issues of member states, such as foreign policy, security, immigration, and police cooperation, remain within the intergovernmental framework of the Council of Ministers, safe from supranational ambitions.[4]

6

The Presidency

Organization

The Presidency is not an EU institution but a distinctive organizational feature that has a bearing on the workings of the Council of Ministers and the European Council, and therefore profoundly influences the outcome, shape, and direction of EU politics. Every six months a different member state takes its turn in assuming the Presidency of the European Union. The order in which this occurs used to be alphabetical, but with the enlargement of 1995 a new system was adopted to balance and reflect the different political and economic characteristics of EU member states. An effort is made, therefore, to rotate the Presidency so that a smaller country is followed by a larger one, and a richer country is preceded by a poorer one, although this formula can only serve as a rough guideline (see Table 6.1). This system might end in 2009, however, should this aspect of the Reform Treaty be taken on board. After 2009, member states therefore might appoint a full-time Council President to chair all summits for two and a half years.

Over the years, the responsibilities of the Presidency have expanded significantly to include:

- preparing and chairing meetings of the European Council
- preparing and chairing meetings of the Council of Ministers and special committees such as the Committee on Budgetary Control
- brokering deals in the Council of Ministers to enact legislation
- launching strategic policy initiatives
- acting as EU spokesperson and representing the EU internationally

These responsibilities can place an enormous strain on the country that holds the Presidency. Large member states have an obvious advantage here, as their sizable bureaucracies offer solid infrastructural support, not to mention the number of civil servants that are required to fulfill such a function. In contrast, smaller countries sometimes have difficulty finding enough qualified people to chair all the meetings. Some member states radically reorganize their bureaucracies in order to absorb the shock of the Presidency, often at the cost of diminished attention to domestic politics. Despite the organizational and administrative burden, small countries relish the chance to be at the helm of EU politics and, understandably, enjoy basking in the international limelight for this period. Regardless of the greater bureaucratic resources of larger states, by no means do they necessarily have more successful presidencies. Another feature of the Presidency is that it can be turned to domestic political advantage either by distracting from pressing problems or by enhancing the government's prestige and popularity.

The Presidency is also responsible for maintaining good relations between EU institutions. Relations between the Council of Ministers and the Commission can be awkward at times, as the latter is a supranational organization designed to promote European integration, whereas the former represents the member states and is designed to safeguard national interests. Yet harmonious relations between the two are crucial for effective policy making, since the Commission proposes legislation that the Council of Ministers (and the European Parliament) subsequently votes on. The Presidency's job, therefore, is to mediate between these two institutions and, if necessary, broker compromises.

The Presidency also plays a role as liaison between the Council of Ministers and the European Parliament. The EP tends to see the Council as the jealous guardian of national sovereignty, and the Council regards the Parliament as the supranational newcomer to the EU's political power game, whose main intention is to increase its legislative and supervising powers. The Presidency has the task of meeting with parliamentary committees and filtering the committees' views back into the decision-making processes within the Council of Ministers.

Although one might argue that the rotating Presidency offers a certain degree of fairness, the system is inherently inefficient, as a term of six months is probably too short to pursue a coherent program. The frequent rotation also undermines political continuity and encourages short-term views and policies.[1] A natural consequence,

Table 6.1. The Rotation of the Presidency

First Half (January to June)	Second Half (July to December)
1996 Italy	1996 Ireland
1997 Netherlands	1997 Luxembourg
1998 United Kingdom	1998 Austria
1999 Germany	1999 Finland
2000 Portugal	2000 France
2001 Sweden	2001 Belgium
2002 Spain	2002 Denmark
2003 Greece	2003 Italy
2004 Ireland	2004 Netherlands
2005 Luxembourg	2005 United Kingdom
2006 Austria	2006 Finland
2007 Germany	2007 Portugal
2008 Slovenia	2008 France

therefore, was that prior to the 2004 enlargement calls for reform were widespread. After all, with twenty-seven members, any given country would hold the Presidency only once every thirteen and a half years, hardly conducive for continuity or political effectiveness. Although the constitution proposed that a president would chair the meetings of the European Council,[2] the principle of a rotating Presidency had not been addressed. A new formula was established taking into account the ten new member states of the 2004 enlargement, and in January 2008 Slovenia was the first of the new member states to assume the Presidency.

7

The European Parliament

Organization

The European Parliament stands out as the only directly elected political body in the EU that has seen its powers increased significantly over the last fifty years. Yet, organizational problems persist, which prompt many analysts to criticize the EU's democratic deficit: the gap in power between executive institutions such as the Council of Ministers, the Commission, and the European Council, on the one hand, and the European Parliament, on the other.

With the accession of Romania and Bulgaria in 2007, the EP had 782 members, elected every five years, with each member state having a specific allocation of representatives. The number of members allotted to each country does not perfectly reflect the size of its population. For example, an MEP from Luxembourg represents sixty thousand fellow citizens, whereas his or her colleague from Germany represents a constituency of around eight hundred thousand. One vital institutional feature of the EP is its party groupings. EP elections consist of twenty-seven parallel elections held in all member states with twenty-seven sets of national parties campaigning for seats. In the UK, for example, competing for seats are British Labourites, British Conservatives, British Greens, and British Liberal Democrats; competing in Germany are

Table 7.1. Party Groupings in the European Parliament, 2004–2009

Party Group	Ideology	Votes
Group of European People's Party and European Democrats (EPP-ED)	Conservatives, Christian Democrats	277
Socialist Group in the European Parliament	Left of center, Social Democrats	218
Group of the Alliance of Liberals and Democrats for Europe (ALDE)	Liberal Democrats, business friendly	106
Union for Europe and the Nations Group (UEN)	Anti-supranationalists but pro EU	44
Group of the Greens/European Free Alliance (Greens/EFA)	Environmentalists and regionalists	42
Confederal Group of the European United Left–Nordic Green Left (GUE-NGL)	Communists	41
Independence/Democracy Group (ID)	Anti-EU	23
Non-attached		34
Total		785

Note: Twenty MEPs are needed to form a party group.

German Social Democrats, German Christian Democrats, German Liberals, and German Greens; and so on. Party groupings therefore try to channel political activity within the EP along sometimes rough political-ideological lines. Table 7.1 shows the respective party groupings for the legislative period of 2004–2009.

The party groups are the organizational vehicles through which the EP functions. They appoint the leaders of the EP and assign speaking times or chair the committees. More important, if a party belongs to a party group, it receives secretarial support, research staff, and financial resources. Parties therefore tend to cobble together, as it is extremely difficult to secure any office or policy goals outside the party groupings.

But although party groupings dominate the EP's daily operations, their importance is severely curtailed, for national parties still largely organize their own electoral campaigns. A Europe-wide party simply does not exist. Also, MEPs come from the national party system, and quite often still think along national lines with their domestic political agenda in mind; some also intend, eventually, to return to their national political scene. Although MEPs are the legislators of European politics, they are still influenced by domestic concerns.

The EP's leadership is comprised of a president and fourteen vice presidents, the latter responsible for chairing meetings and representing the Parliament vis-à-vis other EU institutions. The EP also has a secretariat similar to the Council secretariat and the Commission civil service, offering support services that include research, public relations, and translation. The Parliament also has a committee system that has evolved dramatically over the years, reflecting the increasing impact of the EU on the daily lives of Europeans. For 2004–2009, there are twenty permanent

Table 7.2. Allocation of Seats in the European Parliament

Established at the Nice Summit, 2000			
Old Member States		Post-2004 Accession States	
Germany	99 seats	Poland	50 seats
France	72	Romania*	33
Italy	72	Czech Republic	20
United Kingdom	72	Hungary	20
Spain	50	Bulgaria*	17
Netherlands	25	Slovakia	13
Greece	22	Lithuania	12
Portugal	22	Latvia	8
Sweden	18	Cyprus	6
Austria	17	Estonia	6
Denmark	13	Slovenia	7
Finland	13	Malta	5
Belgium	12		
Ireland	12		
Luxembourg	6		

*Joined the EU in 2007.

committees of varying size and importance,[1] with the job of discussing the legislative proposals that Parliament may vote on during plenary sessions. Two weeks each month are reserved for committee meetings in Brussels that may be attended by Council and the Commission officials, and even, occasionally, other MEPs. Apart from the standing committees, the EP occasionally also has committees of inquiry and temporary committees. This loose structure allows the EP to quickly respond to recent developments that have legislative implications for the EU.

Plenary sessions are the most visible but sometimes the least flattering aspect of the Parliament's work. For a week each month, all MEPs meet in Strasbourg, France. These sessions include debates, speeches by commissioners and by members of the Council Presidency, a question period, and, most important, votes on legislation. The increase in its legislative power has undoubtedly increased the workload of the EP, but occasionally the plenum is sparsely attended, and sometimes the quorum[2] of 393 members required to pass amendments cannot be reached.[3]

The Powers of the European Parliament

As with any national parliament, besides its legislative functions, the EP plays a vital role in the supervision of the executive, the budget, and, to a limited extent, foreign and security policies. With respect to making laws, the history of the EP is one of relentless attempts to increase its institutional power. At the moment, four different paths exist for approving legislation, each giving the EP varying degrees of power. To outsiders these legislative processes can be highly confusing; indeed, most political journalists and, more astonishing, a number of national politicians do not seem to grasp the finer details. But the four paths exemplify the complicated nature of the EU—a carefully struck balance between supranationalism and the power and sovereignty of the member states, a compromise between a union of states and a union of citizens.

All procedures and policies are explained in the treaties and their amendments. The *consultation procedure* was introduced in the Treaty of Rome in 1957. As the name suggests, legislative proposals merely require that the EP is consulted on legislative proposals. The *cooperation procedure*, defined in the Single European Act of 1987, covering, for example, social policy, transport, and the environment, requires that the EP cooperate with the Council of Ministers and the Commission in bringing a legislative proposal to its conclusion; that is, the EP amends a bill on which the Council then has to vote. In this way, the EP sets a conditional agenda, the condition being that the EP gets a proposal from the Commission. The third pathway is the complex *co-decision procedure*, introduced in the Maastricht Treaty, which covers, for instance, the policy fields of health, culture, consumer protection, and the completion of the Single Market. Now the most widely used legislative procedure, if no agreement is reached between the Council of Ministers and the EP, a conciliation committee is formed of members from both institutions to mediate a compromise. If the Conciliation Committee does not reach an agreement, the proposed legislation is abandoned, giving the EP an unconditional veto power. The final procedure is *assent*. Introduced in the Single European Act, a majority of MEPs must agree to accession and association agreements.[4] Parliament has used this power in the past to block certain moves initiated by the Council.[5]

Analysts of the EU's democratic deficit have criticized this system, arguing that it limits the EP's influence on the political process. Obviously, the EP's power is on a sliding scale, from assent and co-decision to consultation. But the EP is not consulted on all legislation. The EP is notoriously weakened, for example, in the area of external agreements. Only two external agreements require the Parliament's approval, the accession of new member states and association agreements. All other acts, such as trade agreements within the WTO, are handled by the Commission with the approval of the Council of Ministers. The EP is informed but no more than that. The same applies to legislation in the area of Justice and Home Affairs.

The EP still has a consultative role in foreign and security policies. The Maastricht Treaty of 1993 dictated that the member state holding the Presidency must consult with the EP on the main aspects and basic choices of the common foreign and security policy, and then ensure that the EP's views are considered. The EP even has a committee that deals with these matters, the Committee on Foreign Affairs and Security. One might argue that this consultative function does not amount to much, but the main achievement for the Parliament is its involvement in a field considered

Table 7.3. Legislative Procedures in the EU

Procedure	Where Introduced	Power of the EP	Policies
Consultation	Rome, 1957	Consultation	Economic and Monetary Union
Cooperation	Single European Act, 1987	Conditional agenda setter	Social Policy, Transport, Environment
Co-decision	Maastricht Treaty, 1993	Veto	Health, Culture, Consumer Protection, Single Market
Assent	Single European Act, 1987	Veto	Accession, Association

to be high politics and of the utmost importance to the member states. This greatly enhances its political stature and impact, as sensitive issues now are given an additional public airing, not only at the national level in national parliaments but, after Maastricht, on the supranational level as well. Still, the power of the EP in these matters cannot be described as comprehensive.

Arguably the EP's most important power is its budgetary authority. The Parliament has exclusive authority to grant a discharge of the general budget by verifying the accuracy of the Commission's budgetary management and determining precise revenue and expenditure. The Parliament regards the discharge option as a potential weapon for censoring the Commission, which it did in 1982 by refusing to accept the budget of Commission President Gaston Thorn. A political crisis was only avoided by the premature departure of Thorn and the inauguration of the Delors administration.

Still, the EP's budgetary power ought to be viewed in perspective. The EU budget is small (recall, it is only around 1 percent of the joint GNP of all member states), and the most politically sensitive expenditure items of a budget—welfare spending, defense, and education—tend to fall outside the scope of the EU and are covered mostly by national budgets. The EP may have acquired budgetary authority, but as long as the budget remains insignificant, and as long as Parliament cannot raise any revenue (for instance, by introducing taxes), its powers in this field will remain rather weak.

The Democratic Deficit and Other Shortcomings

Just as the Commission has no real equivalent in national politics, the EP is often misperceived as the EU's equivalent to a national legislature. Most MEPs and passionate European federalists argue that the role of the EP should be expanded to the status of a proper democratic parliament, with far-reaching legislative authorities. MEPs argue that the current sharing of legislative power within the triangle of the Council of Ministers, the Commission, and the EP limits the democratic legitimacy of the EU.

In a narrow sense, the democratic deficit is the gap between the power of non-elected institutions—the Commission and the Council of Ministers—and that of national parliaments and the European Parliament. The gap results, in part, from the transfer of powers from member states to the EU. Before the transfer, national parliaments held the exclusive power to pass laws. At the EU level, however, the EP shares these powers with other institutions. As the EU acquired greater competence, national parliaments relinquished some of their influence, not just to the European Parliament but also to the Council of Ministers, the Commission, and the European Council.

Nor does it help that the public and the media are quite indifferent to the fact that the only elected body, the EP, has no power to propose legislation. Although MEPs have consistently argued for more power to the EP, the introduction of the co-operation and co-decision procedures did not go far enough to meet their demands. Although these procedures did increase the powers of the Parliament, none granted the power to propose legislation. Anticipating this problem, the member-state governments agreed at Maastricht on several provisions to promote an EU that is closer to European citizens, including voting rights for European citizens in local and European elections, even when living in another EU country, and the public's right to petition the EP on matters of EU competence. The Treaty of Amsterdam also stipulated the gradual phasing out of cooperation and its replacement by co-decision. Only in areas vital to the national interests, particularly EMU, will the consultation procedure be applied. But these provisions still do not set the EP on a par with the powers held by national parliaments.

Despite the calls for increasing the EP's powers, some doubt whether a more powerful EP will solve the problem of the democratic deficit. The introduction of various decision-making procedures, after all, did not bring the EU closer to the people but actually distanced it even more. This, of course, has something to do with the unique nature of the EU, that it is not a state with a clearly defined executive and legislative wing. Moreover, the precise course of the institutional future of the EU is not yet properly set, as supranationalism clashes with intergovernmentalism. Until this debate is settled, improvements in the direction of a proper Europe of citizens will constantly sway back and forth between the jealously guarded powers of national governments on one side and increased transparency of the political process and power to democratically elected institutions on the other.[6]

Unfortunately the performance of the EP is often questioned, and the Parliament can appear to shoot itself in the foot when arguing for greater political power. The work of the EP takes place in three different cities. The secretariat sits in Luxembourg, but general plenary sessions take place in Strasbourg and committee meetings are held in Brussels, with endless numbers of boxes, files, and documents being shipped around Europe. This wastes time and money—indeed, according to estimates, some 200 million Euro per year. Although this is more the fault of the patriotic vanities of France and Luxembourg, who are unwilling to agree to a permanent and complete move to Brussels, the performances of some MEPs also leave something to be desired. Generous travel allowances and occasionally lavish spending patterns by individual parliamentarians has brought much criticism. In trying to solve the problem of the democratic deficit, one needs to recognize that a popular perception about the EP is that the Parliament is not the solution but actually part of the problem.

Apart from the democratic deficit, a number of organizational shortcomings in the EP are not flattering to a presumably democratic polity. First, the EP would be more powerful and more like a national parliament if it had more effective ways of holding to account the executive, and particularly the Commission. As a start, though, since 2004 the Commission President must be approved by a majority of MEPs, although the Commission President is first proposed by the member states. The EP's other controlling powers are the rather extreme mechanisms of dismissing the College of Commissioners or discharging the budget, but neither is designed to have a fine-tuning influence over the executive nor are they conducive to debates and agenda sharing. One solution would be for the EP to directly elect the Commission President, or an electoral college similar to that of the United States could be organized, with national parliamentarians as well as MEPs casting their votes. Some critics argue, however, that such a move would greatly advance the power of the EP over the Commission, and thus severely curtail the Commission's role as an impartial broker in the EU's political processes. The EU would gain democratic legitimacy for the EP but at the expense of the Commission.

Another problem is that the European elections are what political scientists term "second-order national contests"; European voters perceive them as having lesser importance than national elections, resulting in low voter turn-out. In the 2004 elections, only 45.5 percent of EU citizens bothered to vote (which is quite low by European standards), and in some countries, for example, Poland, only one in five voters turned up. Voters in EP elections also direct their dissatisfaction with domestic politics against the ruling party, and the result is that in EU elections governing parties most often lose votes whereas opposition and smaller parties do better than in national electoral contests. Analysis has shown that around 20 percent of voters depart from their usual electoral behavior during EU elections; this produces a rather distorted result and shows that European elections are not necessarily about Europe but more about domestic affairs.

A third weakness is that the style of EU elections is closely related to the European party system, in which transnational party federations coordinate the party groupings through loose arrangements with no coherent program, no party hierarchy, and no annual party conference. Indeed, MEPs are not only elected on a national basis but quite often also act out their national identities. European politics is seen through national spectacles with politicians often addressing national instead of European issues, which are dutifully absorbed by the nationally focused media and public. This phenomenon of an often prevailing national mind-set is counterproductive to the EP's development toward a truly European institution with a truly European agenda. A solution would be to establish genuine European political parties competing over European issues. Only then would competitive party democracy emerge. European voters would decide on the winning coalition, and the coalition's political program would be translated into legislative and executive action. At the moment, however, national parties largely commandeer European elections and treat them as quasi-referendums on national politics, which makes for an incoherent European tapestry and a patchwork of twenty-seven different designs.

8

The European Court of Justice

Organization

Although the ECJ is not explicitly mentioned in the Treaty of Rome, it has twenty-seven judges, one from each member state, who are appointed by each member state government for a six-year term. The treaty only mentions that judges must act independently and past records show that decisions have been reached without national biases. The judges are assisted by six advocates general who consider cases and give opinions for the Court's guidance. Judges are free to accept or reject these opinions, but only rarely do they go against them. The positions of judge and advocate general attract the top individuals in their fields, usually from the upper echelon of a national judicial hierarchy or from academia. Despite the recent criticism of the EU and its institutions, being a judge at the ECJ is still regarded as a highly prestigious job.

The duty of the Court is to interpret and apply EU law.[1] To speed up the process, cases need not be decided in plenary sessions (i.e., with all judges present) but can be decided in chambers, with three or five presiding judges. Full plenary sessions are required when a member state or an EU institution is a party in the case and requests a full hearing. In contrast to the judgments rendered by the U.S. Supreme

Table 8.1. The European Court of Justice

- One judge per member state
- Renewable term of six years
- Six Advocates General who analyze cases more deeply
- Single verdict (no dissenting opinions)

Court, only a single verdict is issued, with no dissenting or concurring opinions. As a result, judgments are sometimes awkward and very diplomatically worded to reflect the different views that may arise.

Sources of EU Law

In reaching a verdict, the ECJ can base its judgment on a number of sources of law that are not necessarily restricted to the EU but apply outside the Union's confines. The sources of EU law include treaties such as the Single European Act, the Maastricht Treaty, the treaties of Amsterdam and Nice, and the three founding treaties of the European Community; European legislation, which is produced within the triangle of the European Commission (which proposes legislation) and the European Parliament and the Council of Ministers (both of which vote on the Commission's proposals); international law; and general principles of law, which are defined somewhat vaguely but typically include the constitutional traditions of member states as well as traditional principles of human rights such as nondiscrimination, proportionality, and legality.

How Do Cases Reach the ECJ?

Individual citizens cannot bring their cases to the ECJ but must first exhaust their national judicial systems. The Treaty of Rome allows lower national courts to seek authoritative guidance from the ECJ; the highest courts of a member state *must* seek this guidance. National courts, therefore, do not interpret EC law but ask Luxembourg for guidance on any aspects of Community law raised by domestic issues. Based on the advice given, the national court considers the case and decides whether the national rule is compatible with EC law. The entire process, called the "preliminary reference procedure," is intended to ensure uniform interpretation and application of Community law in each member state.

With the preliminary reference procedure, the Treaty of Rome established a useful tool for the ECJ to strengthen both Community law and the Court's own role within the political system of the European Community. It also became a way for European citizens to force their national courts to clarify national laws in relation to European laws. In particular, the lower court judges, not the national High Court judges, contact Luxembourg. Some less successful judges conclude that calling for

Table 8.2. How Legal Cases Reach the ECJ

- Referred by national courts
- Actions brought by the Commission or member states against other member states
- Actions brought against EU institutions by other institutions or member states
- Appeals from the Court of First Instance

an opinion from the ECJ is a good way to raise their own profile within their national judicial system. Most judges, in any case, are attracted to the concept of the European Union governed not by economics or politics but by law. Whatever the reasons, over the past five decades, national and European judges have developed a symbiotic relationship, with national judges becoming the upholders of Community law in their own states.

Legal actions that are brought by the Commission or member states against other member states and go to ECJ judges are mainly for failing to fulfill treaty obligations. Actions are also brought against EU institutions by other EU institutions or member states. Two classes of action occur: cases concerning the legality of EU legislation and cases brought against EU institutions for failure to act. A third class of cases has the ECJ deciding on appeals from the Court of First Instance.

The Court of First Instance

By the mid-1980s, the ECJ was seriously overworked. As the caseload increased, the time it took to hear a matter and reach a verdict grew to unacceptable proportions.[2] To relieve the burden of cases, in 1989 a new court was introduced—the Court of First Instance—which hears mainly litigation brought by individuals and companies, as well as competition disputes arising from the ECSC and cases involving employees of EU institutions. Like the ECJ, twenty-seven judges, one per member state, are appointed to the Court of First Instance for a renewable term of six years. As with the ECJ, judges must be independent of national governments and, again like the ECJ, work is usually done in chambers and occasionally in plenary sessions for important cases. But unlike the ECJ, the Court has no advocates general to call upon for assistance and advice, and its decisions can be appealed to the ECJ.

Advancing the Case Law of the EU

For much of its existence, the ECJ was the EU's least-known institution. The major decisions of public interest were taken in the Council of Ministers and the Commission, and so the Court enjoyed a rather quiet existence in the sedate Grand Duchy of Luxembourg. Only gradually did the ECJ manage to make an impact on the non-legal world. Despite the Luxembourg Compromise of the 1960s and the Eurosclerosis of the 1970s, the Court persevered and produced groundbreaking rulings that permanently changed the nature of the Community and paved the path toward greater European integration. A number of landmark cases shaped the legal, and hence the political, essence of the EC.[3]

The first landmark case was in 1963, when the Dutch transport firm Van Gend en Loos brought a complaint against Dutch customs for increasing the duty on a chemical product imported from Germany. The firm argued that the Dutch authorities had breached Article 12 of the EEC treaty prohibiting member states from introducing new duties or from increasing existing duties in the common market. The company claimed protection, citing the direct effect of Community law on national law. The ECJ agreed and ruled that Article 12 had a direct effect because it contained a "clear and unconditional prohibition." The court also ruled that any treaty provision that was "self-sufficient and complete" does not require intervention from national legislators and therefore applied directly to individuals. Even more brash was the ECJ's statement that the EU constituted a new legal order whose subjects were not only member states but also their nationals, who then also enjoyed a set of rights.

Van Gend en Loos and the principle of direct effect would have had little impact if Community law did not supersede national law. Otherwise, the member states would simply ignore the ruling and go about their business as in the past. Although the Treaty of Rome is vague about this, the ECJ did not hesitate to assert its supremacy. The first chance to do so came in 1964, one year after the *Van Gend en Loos* case, with the case of *Costa v. ENEL*. Costa, a shareholder in an electricity company that was nationalized by the Italian government, refused to pay his electricity bill and was taken to court by ENEL, Italy's largest power company; Costa's claim was that the nationalization had infringed upon Community law. The ECJ in its verdict did not question the legality of nationalization, which meant that Costa lost his case, but the Court also pointed to the supremacy of EC law over national law. By signing the Treaty of Rome, the member states had transferred sovereign rights to the Community, and so Community law could not be overridden by domestic legal provisions. Otherwise, the legal basis of the Community itself would have been called into question.

This, of course, did not go down well with some member states. Here one needs to evaluate the significance of *Costa* and *Van Gend en Loos*. Direct effect and supremacy had established a completely new configuration for the national judiciary and, indeed, for national politics. In certain circumstances a member state was no longer completely sovereign, and laws and political programs had to be checked against the principles of a supranational legal order. Obviously, some national courts reacted quite strongly against this kind of encroachment. The biggest threats came in the late 1960s from the supreme courts of Italy and West Germany. In several verdicts they hinted that, because Community law apparently guaranteed a lower standard of fundamental rights[4] than national law, the validity of Community law was called into question.

Table 8.3. The Case of *Van Gend en Loos* (1963)

Dutch company imported chemicals from Germany

Dutch customs added import tax

ECJ response:

- Breach against Article 12, which prohibits member states from introducing new duties or increasing existing duties in the common market

- Direct effect of Community law

- Any treaty provision that was "self-sufficient and complete" requires no intervention from national legislators

- Treaty provisions apply directly to individuals

- Community constitutes a new legal order

Table 8.4. The Case of *Costa v. ENEL* (1964)

Italian government nationalized electricity company

In protest, Costa refused to pay electricity bill

ECJ verdict:

- Nationalization was a legal act; Costa had to pay

- Supremacy of EC over national law

So the match between national courts and the ECJ continued. In 1974, the Luxembourg Court responded strongly in *Nold v. the Commission*. Nold was a coal wholesaler seeking the annulment of a decision by the Commission authorizing the publicly owned Ruhr coal-selling agency to adopt certain restrictive criteria for its supply of coal. This meant that Nold could only purchase coal under the burdensome condition that he suffer a financial loss because he no longer could buy directly from his supplier. Nold claimed that the Commission's decision was discriminating and breached his fundamental rights. The case was dismissed on the grounds that the disadvantages claimed by Nold were the result of economic change and the recession in coal production, and were not related to the decision of the Commission. But Nold had also claimed that the Commission had violated both his proprietary right and his right to the free pursuit of business activity as protected by the German constitution. The ECJ responded to this by stating that fundamental rights form an integral part of the general principles of EC law, and in order to safeguard these rights, the Court is bound to draw inspiration from the constitutional traditions of the member states as well as from international law.

At least in the match-up against national courts the ECJ had won the battle. Since then, national courts have generally and relatively easily accepted Community law, and indeed have become an integral part of the new European legal order by applying EC law to their own domestic cases. Still, sometimes the public and politicians are astonished by the extent to which the Court has established its

Table 8.5. The Case of *Nold v. Commission* (1974)

Coal wholesaler Nold argued for breach of his fundamental rights.

Nold sought annulment of Commission decision authorizing the Ruhr coal-selling agency to adopt restrictive criteria for its supply of coal.

ECJ verdict:
- Nold's disadvantage was the result of economic change, not the Commission's decision
- EC legal order incorporates fundamental rights
- EC law draws inspiration from international law and constitutional traditions of member states

supreme position. An example of the Court's reach is the *Factortame* case of 1991, where, for the first time, the ECJ overruled a British act of parliament. The British Merchant Shipping Act of 1988 had banned Spanish trawlers from fishing in UK waters, and the act blatantly stated that 75 percent of directors and shareholders of vessels operating in UK waters must be British. This was an attempt to stop the so-called quota hopping by Spanish vessels simply by taking a British registration. The Court stated that the Shipping Act contravened Community law. The Treaty of Rome already mentioned the freedom of establishment and the freedom to provide services, and the ECJ expanded this to argue that the UK could not demand strict residence and nationality requirements from owners and crew. This outraged British fishermen and, indeed, also the British tabloid press and the wider public. But in this case Luxembourg proved to be more powerful than the UK Parliament, and, in the process, deeply rocked the British political establishment and its understanding of democracy and sovereignty.

The Impact of Community Case Law

With the two principles of direct effect and supremacy, the ECJ was able to significantly advance the objectives of the Treaty of Rome. The free movement of people, for example, was established in *Van Duyn v. Home Office* in 1974.[5] The famous *Cassis de Dijon* case, in 1979, cemented the free movement of goods.[6] In that case, the ECJ established the principle of mutual recognition, which stated that member states must respect the trade rules of other states and cannot seek to impose their own rules on goods that represented a vital cornerstone in the subsequent development of the Single Market. Regarding social policy, the Court made special inroads on women's rights with the case of *Defrenne v. Sabena* in 1976.[7]

In the wake of these victories by the ECJ, significant shortcomings remain in the development of EC law, notably in the area of human rights. The original Treaty of Rome did not mention fundamental rights, although these are an essential ingredient of any constitutional democracy. In 1986, the preamble of the Single European Act acknowledged the Court's repeated emphasis on fundamental rights by referring to the "member states determination to work together to promote democracy on the basis of fundamental rights recognized in the member state constitutions, in the Convention for the Protection of Human Rights and Fundamental Freedoms, and the European Social Charter." But there was never an explicit charter of fundamental rights. Despite vigorous attempts by the EP, even the Maastricht Treaty did not include a human rights charter but merely an article that the union shall respect fundamental rights, as guaranteed by the 1950 European Convention for the Protection of Human Rights and Fundamental Freedoms. In the prelude to the Nice Summit in December 2000, a panel of appointed experts developed an EU human rights charter, but Britain refused to allow this document to be enforceable under EC law. The Reform Treaty of 2007 finally established a more coherent human rights agenda. The treaty incorporates the Charter of Fundamental Rights into EU law, which lays down the rights that EU citizens already possess (for instance, through the Council of Europe's European Convention on Human Rights or through existing EU law). A further aim of the Charter is to ensure that EU institutions abide by these principles. Alas, Poland and the UK insisted on adding a protocol which clarifies that the Charter does not create any new legally enforceable rights than are already provided in these two countries and that no European court can strike down Polish or British legislation in human rights matters.

Although such cases as *Van Gend en Loos* enunciated an unwritten bill of rights, this process can only be described as, in effect, a constitutionalization of bits and pieces. Despite the undeniable fact that the ECJ took significant steps in the creation of a more complete legal system covering more and more aspects of the lives of European citizens, much remains to be done. First, there is still disagreement over the precise nature of the EU: Is it more an economic union or a political one and, if so, to what extent? Pillars II and III in the Maastricht Treaty (CFSP and Justice and Home Affairs, respectively), largely excluded the ECJ, and experts are still divided over the existence of a European demos, that is, a unified European political people. Some argue that the absence of this demos means that the ECJ can never fully develop a proper citizenship agenda—a complete set of rights and responsibilities of the individual versus the EU. Others argue that the EU ought to establish a citizenship agenda as a precondition for establishing a European demos. As a result, the ECJ is forced to interpret many cases under the principles of the Treaty of Rome, particularly the four freedoms of movement regarding goods, services, people, and capital.

The dilemma is illustrated by *The Society for the Protection of Unborn Children (SPUC) v. Grogan* in 1991. The union of students in Ireland, under their president, Stephen Grogan, had produced a leaflet containing information on abortion clinics in Britain. Some years earlier, the Irish organization Open Door Counseling had provided advice to pregnant women on abortion in Britain, and the Irish Supreme Court ordered it to stop this practice. In 1991, however, this concerned only information, not counseling. The Irish High Court, before passing it to its own Supreme Court, submitted the case to the ECJ asking for advice on whether the provision of

Table 8.6. The Case of *SPUC v. Grogan* (1991)

Irish student organization produced a leaflet containing information on abortion clinics in Britain.

The Irish High Court asked the ECJ whether the provision of abortion is a service that falls under the Treaty of Rome and whether this restriction on information about this service is contrary to Article 59 (free movement of services).

SPUC: abortion is not a service; it is immoral and forbidden by the Irish Constitution.

ECJ verdict:

1. Was abortion a service (Articles 59, 60)? Yes

2. Was the information ban a restriction on services? Yes

3. Was the restriction justified? Yes

4. Should the ECJ review national law for its compatibility with fundamental rights? No

---

abortion was a service that falls under Article 59 of the Treaty of Rome (free movement of services) and whether the restriction in one member state on information about this service was contrary to Article 59. The plaintiff in this case, the SPUC, argued that abortion could not be categorized as a service, since it is simply immoral and, after all, forbidden by the Irish Constitution.

The Advocate General's view was that abortion constitutes a service, and although abortion was forbidden in Ireland, Irish people had a right to obtain information about lawful abortion in other member states, and thus this case was within the scope of EC law. But the Advocate General concluded that an information ban was justified, as it was in the public interest of Ireland, meaning that it would be in accordance with the Irish constitution. The ECJ, however, had a very different view. Although it agreed with the Advocate General that abortion is a service, the ECJ maintained that there was no "economic link" between British abortion clinics and the Irish students, and therefore the case does *not* fall within the scope of EC law. The verdict left the impression that it is very difficult to assess whether a national law falls within the scope of the EC, and that a clear definition of the Court's relationship to the Court of Human Rights in Strasbourg would have offered better guidelines. In *Grogan*, however, the ruling was based on the fact that no commercial link existed between the students and the providers of a medical service. In the end, an economic fact was used to settle an issue of morality and social and human rights. This did not do the case proper justice.

9

Checks and Balances

Checks on the European Court of Justice

Once in place, a court should be able to rule and act as independently as possible in interpreting and applying law. Throughout its existence, ECJ judges in Luxembourg enjoyed a quiet existence outside the political limelight of Brussels. Granted, legal wrangles have occurred with national supreme courts that often criticized the establishment of a superior European legal order by the ECJ's case law, but, from an institutional perspective, no political player in the EU has ever questioned the authority of the ECJ. Given that every member state has to appoint one judge, one could assume that rulings tend to be in line with the national background of the judges. But, as already pointed out, past experience yields the overwhelming impression that judges do not vote in line with any political objectives of their member state governments. The ECJ, therefore, can be described as a beacon of judicial independence, and, as such, it reflects great credit to the European project.

Checks on the European Parliament

As in any democratic system, the parliament is controlled by the citizens who vote the parliamentarians into power. As mentioned above, elections to the EP tend to have a much lower turnout than national elections, often producing different majorities than, for instance, an election to a national parliament would. This inconsistency and unpredictability might not be welcomed by the political elite, but it represents a vital form of direct democracy in a European Union which evidently prefers that EU officials are appointed by national governments rather than by direct public elections. The office of the Commission President is a good illustration of this point. More worrisome, however, are the low voter turnouts; this obviously suggests that the public has little political interest in EU affairs, which certainly undermines the public's influence over the one organization designed to represent the values and standards of the European citizen. As previously mentioned, another hindrance to the performance of the EP is the organizational problems, most notably France's persistence to keep the EP, at least partially, in Strasbourg. A complete relocation to Brussels would certainly improve the political effectiveness of the EP, but such a move would require unanimous agreement within the European Council.

A further problem is that the legislative power of the EP depends on the type of policy that is affected by a legislative proposal. In certain initiatives, such as judicial and police cooperation in criminal and civil matters, the EP is completely excluded from the legislative process. In other areas, such as EMU, the consultation procedure that is applied falls short of any decent democratic system. On such vital matters, the representative organ of the citizens ought to be included more fully in the legislative process. On the other hand, some analysts argue that citizens are indeed represented, although only indirectly, as it is the Council of Ministers that can put its mark on legislation. Individual national ministers, after all, assumed their positions through proper democratic elections. But, following this argument to its logical conclusion, the EP's entire raison d'être could come into question. What is the point of a European Parliament with insufficient powers? Would it not be better to abolish the EP completely, and let national parliaments assume supervisory and legislative functions? At any rate, the European Parliament can have its powers increased only through a treaty change, which happened, for instance, at Maastricht when the co-decision procedure was introduced. But the final wording and approval of a treaty change is undertaken by the European Council, and would twenty-seven heads of government want to increase the powers of the very organization that is supposed to keep them in check on behalf of European citizens?

Table 9.1. The Comitology System

Type of Procedure	Interplay Council/Commission	Policy Fields
Advisory Procedure	Commission free to act	Competition, mergers, state aids
Management Procedure	Commission can enact measures *unless* the Committee opposes the measures with QMV	Agriculture
Regulatory Procedure.	Commission can enact measures *only if* the Committee supports the measures by QMV	customs and tariffs, veterinary and plant health, food safety issues
Safeguard Procedure	Commission has to secure prior agreement from the Council	trade, common commercial policy

Checks on the Commission

Over the years, the EP has significantly increased its controlling powers over the Commission. Although the EP has no voice in determining the exact responsibilities of the individual portfolios, it does have the power to dismiss the entire Commission (by a two-thirds majority vote). Also, as the appointment of the Barroso Commission in 2004 demonstrated, the threat of an embarrassing dismissal can hang powerfully in the air.[1] But the EP cannot dismiss individual commissioners. Once the Commission President starts his five-year term, the Parliament pretty much has to go along with his personnel decisions. As a small token, though, Commission President Romano Prodi (1999–2004) agreed that, at the start of every tenure, every commissioner had to appear before the EP's plenum in Strasbourg for some probative questions.

When implementing legislation, the Commission has to respect the rather complicated *Comitology System*—four types of procedures that are conducted by committees chaired by Commission officials but comprised of national civil servants. The first is the *advisory procedure*, where a committee merely counsels the Commission on rule making. Although the Commission must take the utmost account of the committee's opinion, in reality it is free to enact the measures regardless of the committee's opinion. The advisory procedure is used for such policy areas as competition, mergers, and state aid. Second is the *management procedure*, which is used particularly for the CAP. Here the Commission can enact measures unless the committee opposes them with QMV, in which case the measure will be referred to the Council. The third process is the *regulatory procedure* that initially came about to help manage customs tariffs, veterinary and plant health, and food. It is now applied to a range of harmonization issues, where the Commission can enact measures only if the committee supports the measures by QMV; otherwise the matter is referred to the Council. If this is not complex enough, under the *safeguard procedure*, the Commission can act to protect the interests of the EU or a member state only after securing prior agreement from the Council. These procedures are usually applied

Table 9.2. Who Controls the Commission?

- European Parliament
- Comitology system
- Member states

---

in cases under the EU's trade policy. Finally, the Council of Ministers sometimes decides to exercise implementation powers by itself in highly sensitive areas such as health, financial institutions, and EMU.

Apart from the Comitology System, because of practical necessities, member states exert a degree of control over the Commission. With a staff of only some twenty-four thousand, the Commission does not have its own customs, immigration, or veterinary services, or indeed any other public service that would help give real effect to EU legislation. Instead, the Commission relies heavily on the member states' civil services. Without the existence of national officials, it would be impossible to make the CAP work. Where legislation matters most—in factories, on farms, or at airports—the Commission depends entirely on national officials. This is another indicator of the unique nature of the EU as a complex web of supranational bodies and authorities supported by, and dependent on, national executive powers.

National governments, as noted above, have complete discretion in choosing their commissioners and ought to choose them, as the Treaty of Rome puts it, "on the grounds of their general competence." In reality, however, personal and political considerations determine the appointment as much as ability and merit. Appointments are too sensitive politically and bear too much political influence to be left to such idealist virtues as ability or merit. Indeed, nominees rarely come from outside the governing party. Often candidates are appointed to Brussels as a convenient political solution, since the future commissioner might simply be out of political contention for a domestic post.[2] Should commissioners aspire to a high political office after their stint in Brussels, they ought to be sensitive to domestic political developments and carefully try to avoid antagonizing the national governments that are their future masters.

Without questions, commissioners are subject to intense pressure from their national governments and their national electorate, especially if they intend to return to a domestic political career. A line must be drawn, however, between upholding national interests and taking instructions from national governments. Upholding national interests is not necessarily counterproductive to European integration. The European Union thrives on contributions from several traditions and ideologies, whether economic, social, or political. A commissioner, via his or her member state government, can act as a crucial mediator for policy options that could enrich the Union's agenda.

Table 9.3. Who Controls the European Council?

- Country holding the Presidency
- President of the European Commission
- The public

Checks on the European Council

The European Council was not mentioned in the founding treaties, and so, from a strictly legal standpoint, the Council is not an institution of the EU. Its precise functions have gradually developed over time, and the Maastricht Treaty of 1993 describes the Council as a body above the EU, and therefore not subject to the constitutional checks and balances of the other institutions. Still, three points should be mentioned here.

First, the heads of state have to follow an agenda devised by the country holding the Presidency, and so member states cannot put forward items of their own particular interest but must adhere to the issues identified by the Presidency. In the run-up to these summits there are consultations, even intergovernmental conferences, that prepare and shape the agenda of meetings, but, undoubtedly, the member state holding the Presidency has considerable powers to shape the outcome of any summit.

Second, the Commission presidents and their vice presidents are invited to the summit meetings and, depending on their persona, stamina, and political reputation, can place their mark on negotiations. Jacques Santer (president from 1994 to 1999), Romano Prodi (1999 to 2004), and Jose Manual Barroso (2004 to 2009) found it difficult to make their marks on summits, but Jacques Delors (1984–1994) was able to shape the agenda, at least to some extent. One might recall the now legendary clashes between Delors and UK Prime Minister Thatcher. The summit, then, can be used to great advantage by a talented Commission President to seek support for the Commission's policies among the top power holders in Europe, surely an opportunity that no driven Commission President can resist.

Third, in today's world of intensive media coverage, heads of government and their ministers must always keep an eye on domestic politics and the way potential decisions could be received by the public and electorates. An illustration is the performance of the British prime minister John Major in the 1990s. Trapped by his own Euroskeptic party and at least a partially Euroskeptic public, Major was forced to walk a tightrope between slowing down European integration and promoting economic policies at the EU level. Promoting European integration would have meant antagonizing his party and large parts of the electorate, but resisting European integration would have meant a loss of jobs and, again, a negative reception by parts of the British public. In the end, his tenure was a disaster of unconstructive vacillation without a clear vision of Britain's place in Europe.

Table 9.4. Who Controls the Council of Ministers?

- The public, indirectly, by voting for the head of government, who then appoints the ministers
- Committee of Permanent Representatives (Coreper)

Checks on the Council of Ministers

An indirect control of the Council is exercised by the public of the member states which elects their heads of government, who, in turn, form their cabinets with ministers participating in the respective councils. This, of course, is only an indirect form of control that is exacerbated by the fact that European politics still does not get the same public attention as domestic politics. Neither journalists nor citizens follow the political process in Brussels as closely as they do their national agenda. This gap of information and interest is aggravated when Council meetings are held in private, behind closed doors, without the public or journalists present or with no television coverage, thus hiding European politics from media scrutiny.[3]

One could also argue that Coreper—the Committee of Permanent Representatives—controls the Council, since it sets the agenda and prepares and streamlines proposals for the final decision-making round in the Council meetings. The existence and functions of Coreper are little known outside Brussels. Yet it is extremely powerful group and even more secretive than the Council of Ministers.[4] Coreper's ability to shape the Council's agenda and influence decision making by categorizing items as either A (ready for automatic approval) or B (needs more discussion) illustrates its importance. But this system clearly is not democratic, as Coreper is not accountable to the electorate and inaccessible to the public.

PART THREE

POLICIES

10

The Single Market and Competition

The founding fathers of the European Union envisaged the establishment of a Single Market—the free movement of goods, services, capital, and labor—as a crucial guarantor of peace, stability, and economic progress for a region recovering from the catastrophe of World War II. In the early nineteenth century, the German philosopher Immanuel Kant argued, in Perpetual Peace, that trading nations do not go to war with one another simply because war would have a detrimental effect on profits. More than a century later, the EU's original six member states set out to make Kant's dictum a practical reality. Article 2 of the Treaty of Rome of 1957, which established the European Economic Community (EEC), stated that its purpose was "to promote throughout the Community a harmonious development of economic activities, a continuous and balanced expansion, an increase in stability, an accelerated raising of the standard of living, and closer relations between the states belonging to it." But not until 1993 did the European Union fully realize the objective of the treaty. This chapter analyzes the reasons for this delay, how the European Commission managed to convince the member states of the extraordinary benefits that a Single Market could bring, and whether, ten years on, the initiative lived up to its promises. Areas and sectors currently earmarked for further European integration are also discussed. Finally, one must address the

EU's competition policy which is aimed at preventing the emergence of distortions to the market, either through the establishment of monopolies or oligopolies, or through mergers and state aid. The key issues here include:

1. How does market regulation differ from redistribution?
2. Why has the Commission gained so much power in the regulation of the Single Market?
3. Is the EU competition policy free-market or interventionist?

The Development of the Single Market Program

A truly Single Market would give EU citizens a wide choice of products and services from both their home country and from every other member state. Capital would freely move from banks in one member state to banks in other member states. A completed Single Market would give EU citizens the right to work and live anywhere inside the EU. In envisioning a Single or Common Market, the EU planned to create a European sphere of economic activity that would rise above national regulations. However, events did not go according to plan.

Although by 1968 tariffs and custom duties were all abolished within the EEC, the establishment of the four freedoms long remained an unfulfilled promise. The oil crises of 1973 and 1979, and the subsequent recessions, prompted some member states to adopt protectionist measures to shield their national markets and industries from global and even European competition. In the end, a multitude of different product standards spread across the EU, with different national regulations governing the service sector, restrictions on capital mobility, and different standards for professional qualifications. All these national restrictions made trading across borders, not to mention settling in another member state, a difficult and sometimes impossible exercise. Despite an emphasis on reducing direct barriers to trade, indirect or national actions kept markets highly fragmented.

By the mid-1980s a different global environment forced the EU into a major reevaluation of the potential benefits of a truly Single Market. In the United States, President Ronald Reagan had just embarked on an ambitious defense program aiming to protect the U.S. against nuclear attack by using satellite technology. As a result, military innovation spilled over into the civilian economy, and the U.S. became a global leader in such fields as computer or robotics technology. On the other side of the Pacific, Japan continued to expand its position as the world's leading provider of consumer products, ranging from television and audio equipment to cars. With advancing globalization, however, Europe was seen to be falling behind. Instead of offering products and services across Europe (as the Treaty of Rome had envisioned), industries were often confined to their own national markets which had detrimental effects on innovation, efficiency, and profitability. Against the backdrop of Europe's increasing inability to compete with Japan or the United States, the Commission, as well as several member states (most notably Britain under Prime Minister Thatcher) and large European companies advocated new initiatives.

A significant advance toward a true Single Market was achieved with the Commission White Paper of 1985. The Paper argued for the introduction of Qualified Majority Voting in the Council of Ministers (except on tax issues) so that agreement on certain issues could be achieved more easily than under the previous system of unanimity voting. More important, however, the White Paper planned for the completion of the Single Market by January 1, 1993. All the member states had to do was to implement into law 270 measures that were distributed over three areas: physical barriers, technical barriers, and tax barriers.

Physical barriers, the Commission argued, should not only be reduced but should be eliminated. Goods and citizens should not to be held up at frontiers.[1] Technical barriers, too, should come down; goods should be able to go on sale anywhere in the EC, as long as they were lawfully produced in one member state and the health and safety of the public were not compromised. An exchange of financial products, such as insurance policies, should be made possible, and transport and passenger services, still largely controlled by national governments, should be liberalized. Finally, currencies should move freely across borders, and professional qualifications should be uniform throughout the EU.

With regard to fiscal barriers, the Commission did not argue for uniformity in income or corporate taxes, as any member state's tax system is also a moral value system that societies use to express their objectives. High-tax societies, such as the Scandinavian countries, have reached a consensus to finance public goods (education, transport, health care, and pensions) through the state budget, whereas lower-tax societies, such as the UK under Margaret Thatcher, supported lower state spending and greater individual responsibility. Hence making the tax structure uniform across the EU would mean unifying value systems and societal agreements that have developed over a long period. The Commission, therefore, concentrated mostly on indirect taxation in the form of a value-added tax (VAT) on goods that differed significantly from state to state. With VAT affecting prices, different VAT rates represented a trade distortion. To remedy this, the Commission proposed a narrow band of VAT across the EU of a 5 percent difference between the highest and the lowest rates.[2]

The Benefits of a Single Market

The Commission needed to convince all member states that eliminating national barriers to the four freedoms would ultimately be worthwhile. Indeed, the expected benefits for member states were too significant to resist, and in 1988 a steering group, headed by the senior Commission official Paolo Cecchini, issued a report predicting that the GDP across the EU would rise by 5 percent or more mainly because of lower costs for business transactions. Cecchini also emphasized that the Single

Market would create 2 million more jobs. In that same year the consulting firm Price Waterhouse was even more optimistic, predicting a rise of 7 percent in the GDP, with 5 million more jobs created and a drop in prices of 4.5 percent. The Cecchini Report warned that the failure to implement would cause member states to lose money as a result of extra costs (which Cecchini termed the costs of non-Europe). These extra costs, the Commission bluntly stated, would amount to 200 billion Euros. Against these powerful arguments, national governments would have been foolish if they did not implement the 270 measures and adhere to the seven-year deadline of 1993.

In 2003 the Commission took stock and analyzed whether the Single Market program had really delivered on its promises. In retrospect, the analysis was slightly less optimistic than the Cecchini report, but the results still justified the massive regulatory program. The Commission estimated that, because of the Single Market, in 2002 the GDP was 1.8 percent higher and around 2.5 million additional jobs had been created. These improvements are not necessarily a benefit of the Single Market, however. The first ten years of the Single Market coincided in part with a worldwide economic boom, and it is difficult to judge precisely whether the GDP rise was a result of increased global trade or increased intra-EU trade.

Nonetheless, a final verdict on the success of the Single Market has to mention a number of positive developments. First, the EU continues to witness a large increase in cross-border mergers which testifies to the easing of national regulations regarding the movement of capital. Additional cross-border mergers also indicate that many businesses accept the whole of the EU as their sphere of economic activity. Second, the EU benefited from a massive fourfold increase in foreign direct investment (FDI), which may be regarded as an indicator of the attractiveness Europe now enjoys in the global business community. Third, member states prefer to trade with one another; only 32 percent of the overall EU trade volume is done with non-EU countries, whereas intra-EU trade accounts for 68 percent. Clearly the removal of barriers had worked.[3] Fourth, national firms were clearly oriented toward a more competitive European and global climate. Through the Single Market, companies such as Deutsche Bank, Nokia, and Ciba-Geigy could use their European base as a springboard for entering the global market. Fifth, increased competition led to increased rationalization and economies of scale, resulting in more choice, higher quality, and, above all, significantly reduced prices.[4] And finally, in 2002, 15 million Europeans had taken advantage of the free movement of people and were living in another member state.[5]

A Work in Progress

Although the deadline for establishing the Single Market was at the end of 1992, the EU still produces new legislation aimed at either new product standards or services (such as harmonizing mobile phone technology) or certain sectors that were not addressed previously. By 2002, for instance, the total number of directives related

Table 10.1. Transposition Deficit of Single Market Legislation by Member State
(percent, as of June 2006)

Greece	3.8
Italy	3.8
Luxembourg	3.8
Portugal	3.7
Czech Republic	3.0
Malta	2.2
Belgium	2.0
Ireland	2.0
France	1.9
Germany	1.8
Spain	1.7
Finland	1.5
Netherlands	1.5
Latvia	1.5
Austria	1.4
Estonia	1.4
Poland	1.4
Slovakia	1.4
Sweden	1.4
United Kingdom	1.3
Lithuania	1.2
Slovenia	1.2
Cyprus	1.0
Hungary	1.0
Denmark	0.5

Source: European Commission, Directorate Internal Market, *Internal Market Scoreboard*, no. 15 (July 2006)

to the Single Market had risen to 1,475, with one-eighth of them agreed on between 1995 and 2002.[6]

There always remains outstanding European legislation that still needs to be ratified into national law. Here, the Single Market scoreboard of the European Commission[7] is an effective way to monitor the progress and performance of individual member states by indicating their relative performance in implementing Single Market legislation (see Table 10.1). Applying pressure on the member states has worked well, as the EU average deficit has steadily fallen from 6.3 percent in 1997 to 2.5 percent in 2001. The enlargement of 2004 resulted in a momentary rise to 7 percent, but this dropped to 1.9 percent in June 2006.

The Single Market has had a substantial impact on the liberalization of air transport, triggering the explosion in budget airline services as well as in telecommunications, and, to a lesser extent, in electricity, gas, and railways. The most notable program to close the gap is the *Lisbon Strategy*, which was developed under the Presidency of Portugal in March 2000 to implement economic, social, and environmental renewal by 2010. According to *Lisbon*, the EU aims to become the "world's most competitive and dynamic knowledge-based economy." But in contrast to the U.S., Europe's emphasis will not only be on growth but also on social and environmental cohesion. As targets, *Lisbon* set out an ambitious agenda, illustrated in Table 10.2. As the vehicle for *Lisbon*, the EU agreed on the so-called open-method of coordination, which calls for a collaboration between the twenty-seven member states and the Commission.[8]

Until 2007, however, progress was slow, and some national governments blamed this on the overall economic downturn during the first half of this decade. But one also has to look at the nature of the *Lisbon Strategy*. It was largely associated with the "Anglo-Saxon" model of achieving high levels of employment and growth through deregulation and trade liberalization without worrying much about potential income inequalities. In other words, *Lisbon* was very much about supply-side economic reforms, which contrast sharply with the continental model of economic governance that advocates higher minimum wages, generous welfare benefits, and extensive worker rights, but also suffers from growing unemployment levels. The problem for many national governments in the implementation of *Lisbon* was therefore straightforward. In the age of globalization, politicians are facing an increasingly skeptical public that seems reluctant to give up much of their welfare state. In the spring of 2005 French President Jacques Chirac had already described neo-liberalism (i.e., the Anglo-Saxon model) as the new communism, and it remains to be seen whether continental member states are willing to partially dismantle their own postwar models.

Beyond Lisbon, the Commission set further priorities in its *Single Market Strategy 2003–2006*. The Commission cited the reasons for this initiative as the sluggish progress of Lisbon, the 2004 enlargement, and the current economic malaise, as well as the demographic challenge of an ageing population. The strategy concentrated on the removal of obstacles to trade in goods and services, and on cutting red tape, tackling tax barriers, and expanding procurement possibilities. The priority of establishing an integrated Services Market caused much political controversy in some member states, most notably in Germany and France. The so-called Boltkestein directive[9] aimed at completely liberalizing services across the EU, which provided 75 percent of jobs and 66 percent of the GDP. The Commission argued that freeing this market from national regulations, such as labor laws, registration procedures, and professional standards, would lead to increased competition across borders, followed by better and cheaper services. In reality, this would have meant that a company based in, say, Poland and subject to the domestic labor laws of that country could have made a contract in Germany, for example, and sent its workforce there without being subject to the much more stringent German labor or workplace regulations. Thus some member governments feared that the Boltkestein directive would result in a regulatory race to the bottom, with member states that

Table 10.2. Aims of the Lisbon Strategy, 2000–2010

Liberalize telecommunications, gas, and electricity
Establish an EU wide patent
Liberalize postal systems and rail transport
Rationalize road tax system
Reduce red tape in labor market
Aim for pension portability
Raise employment rate
Harmonize corporation taxes
Promote use of Internet and e-commerce
Complete Single Market in financial services
Open government procurement
Reduce state subsidies

have the least amount of social protection (and therefore the least costs for businesses) gaining a distinct competitive advantage. It therefore came as no surprise that the Commission's proposal was watered down by the member states and by the European Parliament in order to avoid "social dumping."[10]

Safeguarding the Single Market: Competition Policy

A coherent competition policy aims to create a system of undistorted competition between economic players, by preventing monopolies and oligopolies. Competition policy refers to the establishment of fair rules of the economic game, and thus it places constraints on the behavior of economic actors. Exceptions are allowed so as to guarantee the reliable provision of vital goods and services (in the EU, for instance, in agriculture and transport) or to safeguard the public interest (for instance, the restrictive selling of alcohol in Sweden). Monopolies and oligopolies can harm consumers, since a market dominated by only a few players may result in inflated prices and inferior quality. In its efforts to ensure fair competition, EU policy makers are constantly faced with the problem that every member state is responsible for implementing EU policy while at the same time protecting its own national business interests.

EU competition policy is based on a number of treaty and other legal provisions, with the key elements listed in Table 10.3. The Commission's paramount goal is to prevent individual actors or groups of actors from gaining a dominant market position (Articles 82 and 81, respectively), defined as a market share of at least 50 percent. Similar to the U.S. anti-trust laws, the Commission is entitled to impose restrictions on economic actors. For example, the Commission imposed a fine of 75 million Euros on the Swedish company Tetra Pak, one of the world's market leaders in packaging liquid foods, with an EU market share of 95 percent, for unfair marketing, contract, and pricing policies.

Table 10.3. The Competition Policy

Treaty Article 81: agreements between undertakings (i.e., companies) which may affect trade between member states *and* which have as their object or effect the prevention, restriction, or distortion of competition . . . are prohibited.
Treaty Article 82: Any abuse by one or more undertakings of a dominant position . . . shall be prohibited.
Regulation 1/2003 (formerly known as 17/62): The Commission is responsible for ensuring Articles 81 and 82.
Treaty Article 86: extends Articles 81 and 82 to public enterprises.

EU Competition policy has correctly been defined as the "first supranational policy,"[11] as it grants member states limited advisory capacity in the Commission's executive decisions. By 2000, the European Commission's caseload had grown so heavy that Regulation 17 was reformed to include the application of European law by national authorities and a shift from a before-the-fact notification procedure to an after-the-fact control system. This meant that national competition authorities became highly "Europeanized" as agencies operating under European law, and that the European Commission would concentrate its resources on "hard-core" cases while monitoring the application of European law among national competition authorities.

Avoiding Market Dominance: Merger Policy

Established in 1989, the EU's merger policy is complicated by the fact that mergers at a national level are organized according to different national rules. The body ruling over mergers in Germany, for instance, is politically independent, and its decisions are rarely overruled. Rulings in the UK, in contrast, are made by a governmental institution, the Department of Trade and Industry. Hence the Commission investigates only mergers that affect enterprises across borders, and it bases its rulings on whether effective competition is preserved (i.e., whether a dominant market position of 50 percent or more might be established as a consequence of the merger), while acknowledging other factors such as technological development and economic progress.

The fall of national barriers as a result of the Single Market program, along with the introduction of a single European currency, has caused a steady rise in the number of mergers. Between 1990 and 2002 the Commission issued verdicts on 2,047 cases, but it only blocked 22 and saw 80 potential mergers abandoned during the Commission's review. In 1994, for instance, the Commission blocked the merger of Deutsche Telecom, Bertelsmann (one of the world's biggest media providers), and Kirch (a German pay TV company) on the grounds that the new company, MSG Media Service, would gain a dominant market position for pay TV and cable networks. On the other hand, in 1992 the Commission approved the merger of Nestlé and Perrier, but only after Nestlé agreed to surrender control of 20 percent of the French mineral water market.

Keeping a Level Playing Field: State Aid Provisions

As a general rule, state aid, or the financial support of private or public enterprises through public funds, usually distorts competition, since publicly funded economic players generally have a competitive advantage over those not receiving public assistance. Article 87 has provisions, however, that allow companies to receive financial support from the state or publicly owned organizations. These provisions allow public funding under the following circumstances:

- The state aid has a social character and is granted to an individual without discrimination against others.
- The state aid compensates for damage caused by natural disasters.
- In the case of eastern Germany, state aid is granted in order to overcome the economic and social disparities between the former communist eastern and the western part.

Other exceptions may be made when aid would promote the economic development of an area with a low standard of living, execute an important project of common European interest, or, as a final legislative loophole, promote certain economic activities.

State aid is widespread and accounts for around 100 billion Euros annually. The Commission receives about six hundred notifications and investigates another one hundred unregistered cases but rarely voices any objections. Reasons often cited for providing state aid are economic circumstances such as the preservation of jobs, or when the aid contributes to EU objectives such as environmental protection, and social and regional cohesion. The Commission put its foot down, though, in the case of the French government and its financial support of 3.5 billion Euros for Air France in 1994. Because the airline was a prestigious symbol of French national pride, the Commission had to carefully avoid antagonizing one of its key allies in the drive for further European integration. However, DG Competition, which takes decisions on competition law cases including infringements, mergers, and state aid, ruled that this cash injection had to be the last of its kind and imposed the condition that the money could only be used for restructuring purposes, not for anti-competitive measures such as ticket price cuts. Despite the restrictions, the ruling outraged private airlines, most notably British Airways.

Why Care about the Single Market?

A number of key debates that must be kept in mind when assessing information on the Single Market can be grouped under four general issues.

Issue 1: Why did the Single Market program happen in the mid-1980s? As noted above, the Single Market program, as well as the Single European Act that laid the institutional foundations for economic policy reform, emerged in the context of different interests demanding liberalization of trade between member states. For some, the Single Market initiative represents a major triumph for the European Commission in that it served as a "policy entrepreneur" in shaping the agenda and pushing it through. Others point to the considerable importance of big business, which demanded not only a single market but also the development of a merger policy regime designed to resolve previous legal uncertainties. In many ways, the Single Market program targeted especially those sectors where trade flows across national borders were particularly high. And, finally, for some the Single Market program represents little else than the convergence of national political preferences. These debates point to the different governmental approaches in Germany, the UK, and France, suggesting that the Single Market, in various ways, extends domestic economic policy agendas as well as responses to domestic business demands.

Issue 2: The EU as a regulatory state. Regulation is the key mode of governance in the European Union. Rules give member states and businesses a predictable foundation on which to base their transactions, while they are monitored by a "neutral referee" (i.e., the European Commission). Like any organization, however, the Commission has its own self-interest. Within the EU's institutional setup, the Commission has very little power to demand additional financial resources, and even where it has appropriate funds, these remain largely connected to highly fixed agricultural schemes. Given this lack of financial muscle to shape policies, the Commission has used regulation in an attempt to maximize its power.

Issue 3: Deregulation or re-regulation? Many have feared the deregulatory consequences of a Single Market. In many ways, this refers back to the old dualism of the supranational character of EU law, which emphasizes economic freedoms versus intergovernmental policy making that blocks attempts at "positive integration."[12] The big question, then, is whether the Single Market advanced the cause of negative integration over positive integration? At first sight, one should expect this to be the case. What is widely known as the Delaware effect predicts that member states will seek to attract industry by offering a low-cost base for production. Firms will therefore move to the place where they can produce in the cheapest possible manner. As all member states compete to attract investment, a spiral of deregulation emerges, resulting in a "race to the bottom." But such a race has hardly been in evidence. Instead, what has emerged are relatively high environmental standards, owing particularly to the political preferences of large and rich member states, as well as "product standards" that visibly alter the quality of the good being produced. Even the area of "process standards," such as labor regulation, has witnessed an emphasis on defining minimum standards rather than a race to the bottom. The picture that emerges from the different sectoral experiences is actually one of far higher diversity than a simple "negative" versus "positive" integration argument would suggest.

Issue 4: What has been the impact at the national level? The evidence from across policy domains and member states suggests that there has been considerable and persistent diversity rather than a "convergence" of different starting points toward a unified policy. As shown in Table 10.1, some member states have proved resistant to the complete implementation of the Single Market program. Also, member states have sometimes applied substantial creativity in interpreting EU law. For example, EU law that was meant to liberalize road haulage across member states led Italy to take a far more restrictive approach to cross-border traffic. These experiences suggest the pivotal importance of national administrations in interpreting and implementing EU law in their own jurisdictions.

Conclusion

The Single Market, one of the key achievements of the European Union, has largely been a program of "re-regulation" and not "de-regulation." Even measures that have supported the liberalization of economic activities, such as increased competition in telecommunications, require a substantial number of rules, in many ways even more rules than the previous age of protected national markets. In this regime of "re-regulation," the European Commission has played a substantial role as policy entrepreneur in shaping the policy agenda and seeking to maximize its influence over the substance of policy. Finally, the Single Market has not led to uniform economic policies across member states or policy domains. Far from it; indeed, the economic landscape is characterized by a regulatory patchwork with different member states choosing different strategies to respond to the Single Market and with the European Commission choosing different strategies for different policy domains. In many ways, the Single Market continues to be far from single.

11

Regional Policy and Cohesion

Cohesion intends to close the prosperity gap between rich and poor, or, more specifically, is the process of reducing economic and social disparities between regions. The EU has 268 regions, 81 in the 12 new member states and 187 in the old EU-15. Some regions are simply synonymous with established historical entities, such as Catalonia in Spain, Tuscany in Italy, or Bavaria in Germany, but regions had to be created in countries without a federalist tradition, such as the UK. Thus Britain has the South-West region, which has no historical precedent. A region ought to represent a coherent, geographical, administrative, and, above all, economic entity. The EU measures the wealth of a region based on its GDP per capita. Three questions surround the current picture of cohesion:

1. Is EU cohesion simply a side-payment to buy support for European integration?
2. Has EU cohesion reduced economic disparities in the EU?
3. Should the EU be concerned with cohesion at all?

The Rationale behind Cohesion

There are three reasons why cohesion represents a desirable goal for any given society. First, from an economic perspective, in a liberal market economy, market forces alone cannot solve long-standing regional problems; the market will always go where the most affluent consumers are and where the highest profit margins are to be expected. Across Europe, one often sees a core with a very active and success-ful economy surrounded by a periphery, which is incapable of reaching comparable standards of living. Underutilized resources in the periphery, mainly human capital, could significantly contribute to growth and productivity if used more efficiently, which is the precise aim of cohesion. Second, from a social perspective, attempts to reduce the long-standing trend of people moving away from the periphery and into core urban areas could result in fewer urban problems, including overcrowd-ing, traffic congestion, or crime. Moreover, efforts to preserve rural communities, and cultural and social traditions, seem worthwhile against the backdrop of the streamlining trends of globalization. And, third, from a political perspective, one might argue that every member of a society should have the possibility of sharing a country's wealth. Any political system able to distribute wealth in a just manner will enhance its democratic legitimacy.

Why should the European Union tackle such idealistic objectives? Cohesion and closing the gap between rich and poor would result in a more unified Europe, which is certainly in line with the ideals that brought the European project into ex-istence some fifty years ago. Cohesion could also compensate for the negative effects of other EU policies, particularly the Common Agricultural Policy which mainly benefits large-scale producers, whereas the small-business farmers, so prevalent in Greece, Ireland, Spain, Southern Italy, and Portugal, find it hard to achieve ac-ceptable standards of living. Another example is the Single Market Initiative; ever since the Single European Act was signed in 1986, economic activity has tended to concentrate on the so-called blue banana,[1] with outer lying regions missing out. On the other hand, growth and economic prosperity in disadvantaged regions would lead to reduced unemployment and higher tax revenues for the state. And because the EU budget is the sum of national contributions in the region of around 1 percent of every member state's GDP, the EU has a vested interest in spreading prosperity. Most important, though, is who but the EU would be in the position to tackle cohe-sion? With bilateral aid the exception rather than the norm, poorer member states and their regions depend on support from Brussels.

How Does the EU Implement Cohesion?

Cohesion is organized around a number of funds and the process can get compli-cated, as often happens when money is at stake. Any investigation of how cohesion works will encounter a multitude of funds, some with confusing names and most of them with unique program objectives and their own bureaucratic jargon.

Table 11.1. Financial Breakdown of the Cohesion Policy, 2007–2013

Objective	Share	Amount (in billion Euros at 2004 prices)
Convergence	81.9%	252.349
Regional Competitiveness and Employment	15.7%	48.375
Territorial Cooperation	2.4%	7.395
Total		308.119

Source: European Commission, Directorate Regional Policy.

In making its financial projections for 2000–2006, the EU's cohesion policy did not properly address the integration of twelve new and largely poor countries. With the enlargement rounds of 2004 and 2007, the current multi-annual budget for 2007–2013 had to consider the vastly changing circumstances of a union that had never before witnessed such a wide gulf in prosperity and development. In July 2004, the Commission published its first proposal arguing for funding to be concentrated only on the neediest regions. Brussels argued for an increase to 336 billion Euros—about one-third of the EU's budget—which was still only the same share spent on cohesion in the previous financial projections for 2000–2006. In addition, the Commission intended to simplify the program structure by dividing the entire pot of money into three distinct spending categories.[2]

The European Council meeting of December 2005 largely approved the Commission's proposal. After much negotiating, the member states agreed to set a financial ceiling for cohesion at 308.119 billion Euros, a little less than the Commission wanted. Cohesion in the EU is now allocated to three areas:

- 81.9 percent is for Convergence projects in the poorest regions to reduce the gap between the poorer and richer regions[3]
- 15.7 percent is for Regional Competitiveness and Employment projects related to innovation, sustainable development, greater accessibility, and job-training projects[4]
- the remaining 2.4 percent goes to European Territorial Cooperation projects to achieve broader cooperation between frontier regions, including regions bordering non-EU territory[5]

A further simplification was to reduce the number of financial vehicles to three: the European Regional Development Fund (ERDF), the European Social Fund (ESF), and the Cohesion Fund.[6] The ERDF is used to reduce regional disparities by supporting research, innovation, environmental protection and risk prevention, with the strongest emphasis on infrastructure. The ESF focuses on human resources by promoting skills, access to and participation in the labor market, and

Table 11.2. The EU's Budget, 2007–2013 (in billion Euros)

Budget Heading	Purpose	Total
1A: Competitiveness for Growth and Employment	Lisbon Strategy, research and technology, education and training, nuclear de-commissioning	72.010
1B: Cohesion for Growth and Employment	Cohesion Policy	308.119
2 Preservation and Management of Natural Resources	Agriculture, rural development, fisheries, and environment	252.460
3A: Freedom, Security, and Justice	Asylum, immigration, border control, cross-border problems, terrorism, organized crime, judicial cooperation	6.630
3B: Other internal policies	Culture, youth, audiovisual matters, health, and consumer protection	3.640
4. The EU as a global partner	Global security, pre-accession stability, development and economic cooperation, European neighborhood, humanitarian aid macro financial assistance	50.010
5. Administration		50.300
Others		122.194
Total		865.363

social inclusion. The Cohesion Fund is exclusively for poorer member states with a GDP of less than 90 percent of the EU average;[7] together with the ERDF, the fund contributes to multi-annual investment programs in transport infrastructure and environmental protection.

How Is Money Distributed?

Cohesion in the EU requires that all projects adhere to four principles, regardless of the fund they relate to. These include:

1. *Additionality.* The funds must be used in addition to existing national cohesion initiatives, and not to replace national cohesion policies.
2. *Partnership.* Projects must be managed within the triangle of the Commission, regions, and national governments.
3. *Programming.* Funding must be delivered through multi-annual development programs. One-off funding for projects does not exist. Instead, specific projects must fit into a wider strategy.
4. *Concentration.* Funds must be spent primarily on areas that fulfill one of the three objectives of the structural funds, namely, to concentrate resources on regions with the greatest needs.

Arguably the most crucial player in the distribution of financial support is the Council of Ministers, which determines the allocation of funds and the policy objectives. It also sets the financial limits and decides, in often acrimonious debates, how much money each member state will receive.[8] The responsibility for getting projects started, however, rests with each region, which first has to design the project, identify partner organizations, develop an implementation plan, draft a budget, and then lobby its national government to approve the project. The project is then passed to the European Commission, which starts a close dialogue with the regional authorities over funding, organization, and planning.[9]

It is important to realize that the EU does not entirely fund projects but only offers to make up the needed difference. A considerable share of the costs must be met by local, regional, or national sources, and most projects receive a contribution from Brussels of around 50 percent. When assessing the projects, the Commission checks on a number of criteria that can make or break a proposed project. A project ought to create long-term, sustainable *jobs*. It also should improve the overall *infrastructure* of a region, not necessarily just through roads, harbors, airports and rail links but also by improving communication. All this, of course, must be done in a manner that does not harm but might even improve the *environment*. Projects offering *economic diversity* by integrating elements of business, civil society, and academia will also improve their prospects for funding. Finally, the criteria of *competitiveness* and *enterprise* are applied to cutting-edge projects using novel ideas and new approaches that will have long-term commercial viability.

The Challenge of Enlargement

With the accession of twelve new member states in 2004 and 2007, the EU population grew by 128 million people, or around 32 percent, to 485 million. These new EU citizens are in regions with a GDP of less than 75 percent of the EU average, thus falling under Objective One status. But even among the new member states, a widespread gap exists between, for instance, Cyprus, with 70 percent of the EU's average prosperity levels, and Bulgaria and Romania, with about 30 percent. With the integration of Bulgaria and Romania, the EU's GDP per capita had actually dropped in 2007 by around 18 percent relative to the EU's original fifteen member states. Given this widened cohesion gap, it seemed astonishing that the EU made no special arrangements when the financial perspective of 2000–2006 was agreed upon at a summit in Berlin in March 1999. Back then, enlargement was still deemed to be a distant possibility. In fact, the EU-15 was under the impression that, if any countries would be added, maybe only five candidate countries (Poland, Hungary, the Czech Republic, Estonia, and Slovenia) would make the grade in the medium-term future. In Berlin, therefore, the member states agreed to offer relatively modest financial assistance, delivered through various programs, amounting to 21.8 billion Euros for the years 2000–2006, or around 3 billion Euros per year.[10] Already prior to Berlin, Europe Agreements had been signed with all candidate countries to gradually establish free trade and to monitor the implementation of the acquis communautaire. The candidate countries were also offered participation in existing EU programs for education, training, the environment, transport, and research. Brussels also established the Technical Assistance Information Exchange Instrument (TAIEX), which delivers information on all aspects of the acquis communautaire through seminars and conferences. Finally, a twinning program was launched, in which member states offered the secondment of their civil servants and advisers to the accession countries.

By 2002, however, it became clear that the surprisingly speedy progress of the candidate countries would permit ten states to join in 2004. The EU therefore was forced to somehow find the resources in its current seven-year budget to establish further financial programs. At the Copenhagen summit in December 2002, the member states agreed on a new financial formula and increased the total volume of funds available to the candidate countries to 9.9 billion Euros in 2004, which rose to 14.9 billion in 2006.

Does the Cohesion Policy Work?

Cohesion in the EU is torn between politics and policies. In policy terms, funding should be focused on backward areas requiring support. But politics dictates that cohesion must be supported by a majority of member states. Thus we find a wide range of funding that covers more than 50 percent of the EU-15's population, prompting observers to remark that the Cohesion Policy gives "something for everyone." The policy problem, however, is substantial. Before the enlargement of 2004, 22 percent of EU citizens (some 80 million people) lived in regions with a GDP of less than 75 percent of the EU average, but, with enlargement to Central and Eastern Europe, economic disparities increased even more, to the point where over 30 percent of EU citizens now live in areas with Objective One status. Regarding employment, the extreme differences between regions are illustrated by the mere 2 percent unemployment rate in the prosperous Austrian Tyrol compared to more than 26 percent in the Polish region of Lubuskie. Clearly cohesion in the post-enlargement era is more of a distant objective than a tangible goal.

Nonetheless, evidence also suggests that, undeniably, cohesion is increasing in the EU, though very slowly—at about 2 percent per year. Completion of the Single Market has led to, and will continue to spur, increased specialization. Poorer regions in this respect will benefit from the competitive advantage of having lower wages and production costs. Ireland is often cited as an example where cohesion policy is widely seen as a major reason for the country's astonishing economic success. When Ireland joined the EU in 1973, its GDP languished at 64 percent of the EU's average. Today its GDP is over 130 percent of the EU average, among the highest in the Union.

The remarkable case of Ireland, however, might not be enough to convince the critics of cohesion,[11] who argue that cohesion remains only wishful thinking given both the increasing North-South divide within the old EU-15 and the persistent West-East divide between old and new member states. On top of these divisions, today Germany, Denmark, and France, in particular, have less inner cohesion—the prosperity gap within a member state—than in the past, and the years have seen increasing gaps between richer and poorer regions in Britain, Greece, and Italy. Whereas the pro-cohesion camp cites Ireland, cohesion skeptics present the case of Greece, which in 1983 had a GDP of 62 percent of the EU average and by 2003 the figure had improved only marginally to 65 percent. Unemployment, too, remains a widespread problem, not only in some regions of the 2004 and 2007 accession states but also in Greece and Spain. After all, how can funds that only amount to 30 billion Euros combat such widespread social malaise in the face of the persistent pressures of automation and globalization?

It remains difficult, then, to determine the success of cohesion, since economic progress is influenced significantly by non-EU factors. Again, the case of Ireland offers insight into some of these factors. As noted, Ireland is often portrayed as the champion of cohesion: a country that was propelled from the economic backwardness of the seventies to become the Celtic tiger of the nineties. Ireland, though, is an English-speaking country that even before EU money began pouring in had low wage levels and a highly educated workforce; these factors, in the age of globalization and the European Single Market, are highly conducive to business and foreign investment, apart from any EU cohesion policy. Clearly, then, cohesion and economic success not only depend on a well-managed and coherent allocation of funds from Brussels but also on efficient coordination between the EU and national and regional authorities, as well as on sensible macro-economic policies and a favorable international economic climate.

Even enthusiasts of the EU's cohesion policy cannot ignore the challenge posed by the core-versus-periphery problem. Economic activity in the EU remains centered on the blue banana, the area marked by low assembly costs, an affluent consumer base, good market access and transport links, and the presence of multinational companies, all of which allows for brisk intra-industrial trade. In contrast, the EU's periphery is characterized by a lack of competition, with detrimental effects on labor skills and infrastructure. Also, labor migration in the EU will never reach U.S. levels, which means that any competitive advantage in the periphery (lower wages, lower taxes) might not lead to economic gains. The periphery might always be engaged in a permanent game of catch-up. Projects to improve the infrastructure of the periphery will undoubtedly move it closer to the richer European markets of the center, but in an EU of twenty-seven members stretched across the map of Europe, and with the existing sizable gap between rich and poor, the cohesion policy in the EU still has a long way to go before it can fulfill its laudable objective.

12

The Common Agricultural Policy

From its beginnings in the 1950s the Common Agricultural Policy was a cornerstone of European integration, yet it has always been severely criticized. At first glance it seems odd that a program providing for only 2 percent of the EU's GDP and employing only 5 percent of its workforce should swallow up nearly half its budget. Ever since 1967, when for the first time we had free trade in practically all agricultural products across the European Community, the CAP has been censured for being a uniquely wasteful bureaucratic way of supporting agriculture, and for being managed on the basis of endless negotiations between national ministers who themselves are subject to fierce lobbying. Critics point out that this system, which gives direct subsidies to farmers and sets artificially high prices, shields farmers from market discipline and prevents products from selling more cheaply at world-market prices. Euroskeptics have a great deal of ammunition here in depicting the EU as an overly bureaucratic and inefficient exercise; indeed, CAP even appears to be unnecessary in view of the economic insignificance of European agriculture in the twenty-first century. Yet every EU citizen directly and indirectly supports it—directly through EU payments to farmers and indirectly by paying food prices that in the past were up to 40 percent above the world-market level. So a fundamental question is why the EU's founding fathers decided to support what appears to be institutionalized madness. The key issues in this controversy revolve around the following questions:

1. What are the CAP's key structural design faults?
2. Who are the CAP losers and beneficiaries?
3. Why has the progress of CAP reform been so slow?
4. What challenges did the 2004/2007 enlargement pose for the CAP?

Reasons for Organizing Agriculture

In the run-up to signing the Treaty of Rome, a number of political conditions favored the adoption of an agricultural policy. First, in the early 1950s, some 25 percent of the total workforce of the original six member states was employed in agriculture. In Italy the figure was close to 40 percent, and in France 26 percent. Although in West Germany it was only some 20 percent, farmers represented a major constituency of the ruling Christian Democrats.

Second, except for Luxembourg, the original member states already had a system of farm-price support. Especially in France, West Germany, and Italy, most farmers were small holders and required subsidized prizes to maintain an acceptable level of income. But against the backdrop of the establishment of a European Single Market in 1957, a unified and streamlined agricultural market was therefore simply a necessity.

The third reason was the insistence of the French government, which was prepared to get the European project off the ground only if a strong and durable system of support for prices and farm incomes was developed. France regarded the CAP as a powerful counterweight to the perceived industrial dominance of West Germany within the Community. If Germany, with its strong export-oriented industry, was to benefit from the free movement of goods, the French farmers ought to benefit from a European agricultural policy.

Fourth, in contrast to any industrial sector, the production of many agricultural commodities is subject to forces beyond human control such as droughts, earthquakes, floods, and pests. Obviously, agricultural production is difficult to plan or predict under these randomly occurring natural circumstances. In 1952 the Dutch Minister of Agriculture Sicco Mansholt stated that the principle of economic liberalism (by which he meant the forces of supply and demand) may be suitable for industrial sectors of the economy but it cannot be applied to farming.

Fifthly, agricultural products have low income elasticity of demand. A company such as Sony, for instance, can constantly reinvent its product line. In consumer electronics, for example, the Walkman was followed by the Discman and the portable DVD player. Farmers have very limited opportunity to expand their product line. Simply put, a consumer can buy both a Discman and a DVD player, but one is not inclined to eat two meals instead of one at dinnertime. As general prosperity

Table 12.1. Objectives of the CAP

• Increase agricultural productivity
• Ensure a fair standard of living for farmers
• Stabilize markets
• Assure food supplies
• Provide consumers with food at reasonable prices

Source: Article 39, Treaty of Rome (1957).

levels rise, consumers spend smaller proportions of their income on agricultural products, and so farm incomes tend to lag behind the incomes of those working in the industrial sector.

The Objectives of the CAP

Based on these political, structural, and welfare ideological points, the original six member states spelled out the objectives for the CAP in Article 39 of the Treaty of Rome; the goal was to increase agricultural productivity, ensure a fair standard of living for farmers, stabilize markets, assure food supplies, and provide consumers with food at reasonable prices. On close inspection, two of these goals contradict each other. A fair standard of living for farmers clashes with the objective of providing reasonable prices for consumers. Because farmers receive a substantial portion of their income through food prices, the higher the prices, the higher their standard of living.

How Does the CAP Work?

As a system of indirect income support for farmers, the CAP functions by separating the European Union's internal market from the world market. This is accomplished through three measures:

1. A unified market: the free movement of agricultural products across all borders within the EU
2. Community preference: EU products are preferred over imports from non-EU countries
3. Financial solidarity: the CAP is exclusively funded from the EU budget, and national governments are not allowed to subsidize farmers' income

Even better for European agriculture, every product is guaranteed a price that is higher than the world-market price set annually by the Council of Agriculture Ministers through unanimous voting.[1] The EU also buys any crop surpluses from European farmers, and it imposes a duty on non-EU producers to bring the prices of their

Table 12.2. Pricing System of the CAP

- Target price: guarantees EU farmers a minimum price for every product
- Intervention price: the price at which CAP agencies buy off surplus products (same as target price)
- Entry price: the price that EU importers have to pay (higher than target price)
- Levy: the duty on EU imports that raises them to the level of the target price
- Refund: given to EU exporters to bridge the gap between high EU prices and lower world market prices

---

products from the (lower) world-market level to the (higher) EU level. In return, EU producers receive an export subsidy that brings the cost of their products down from their (higher) EU standard to the (lower) world-market standard. This organizational structure requires the member states to set up agencies that pay farmers for their products, and also buy food surpluses. Member states forward the amount of their CAP expenses every month to the Commission for reimbursement.

The Structural Shortcomings of the CAP System

The most obvious problem here is that guaranteed prices bear no relation to demand, and they encourage overproduction. The more the farmers produce, the more the EC will buy from them.[2] Indeed, between 1973 and 1988, the price guarantees stimulated agricultural production at a rate beyond what the European market could absorb.[3] This led to the problem of having to store the surpluses, some of which are perishable and need refrigeration, thus adding an additional burden to the taxpayer. A further unwanted effect of the CAP is that in attempting to support small, often family-owned farms, the system does exactly the opposite: because the CAP rewards are based on quantity, the greatest beneficiaries are big farmers who have the finances to invest in new technology and equipment.[4] The environment, too, suffered, as farmers, in order to produce more, have the incentive to use pesticides and artificial fertilizers. Finally, Community preference imposes protectionist measures—import taxes and quotas on non-EU farmers—that conflict with the trend toward global free trade, competition, and market liberalization, while export price supports distort world prices, undercut non-EU farmers, and lead to trade disputes and serious disadvantages for developing economies. Admittedly the EU gives much of its food surplus to the underdeveloped world, accounting for over 70 percent of the world's food aid; but although this may be laudable, the CAP still denies producers from developing countries access to rich European markets. Even worse, the dumping of overproduction on Third World markets robs local farmers of the incentive to be self-sufficient and to find their market niche. Picking up an EU food parcel from the aid agency seems much easier than carving out a meager existence by working one's land.

Table 12.3. Shortcomings of the CAP

- Overproduction
- Storage
- Benefits big farms, not small ones
- Environmental damage
- Trade protectionism
- Disincentive for farmers from the developing world to become self-sustaining

---

In the 1970s, the increasing financial burden of the CAP left the EU facing the prospect of bankruptcy. With unlimited market guarantees and increased productivity, and prompted by technical progress, expenses grew as high as around 70 percent of the EU's budget by 1984. Overproduction reached obscene proportions. In the early 1990s, for example, the EU of twelve member states produced 20 percent more food than it could consume, resulting in the infamous wine lakes and the butter and sugar mountains.[5] Clearly something had to be done.

Attempts to Reform the CAP

Given the fundamental problems of the CAP, politicians had a limited number of options for remedying the growing concerns. These include:

1. Reduce prices for consumers
2. Establish production ceilings to lessen overproduction
3. Create land set-aside programs to reduce production
4. Direct payments to poorer farmers to satisfy welfare considerations
5. Set a maximum ceiling of financial support for richer farms
6. Establish environmental standards
7. Allow non-EU farmers access to EU markets and limit export subsidies for EU farmers

Every reform idea used a combination of these solutions to different effect. As a first serious attempt, the European Community introduced the so-called Stabilizer Reform Package of 1988. Initial negotiations were complicated by two opposing fundamental conceptions on how agriculture should be managed. On one side, Britain and Denmark argued for budgetary adjustments, production ceilings, and a producer's tax to help defray the cost of storage and export subsidies. On the other side, Belgium, France, Germany, and the Mediterranean countries emphasized the socio-cultural necessity of supporting agriculture, and argued for continued price support at current levels, with producers suffering only marginal penalties for going over their production ceilings.[6]

Table 12.4. Problems and Solutions for the CAP

Problems	Solutions
High prices	Lower prices
Overproduction	Production ceilings
Storage	Land set-aside programs
Environmental damage	Direct payments to poorer farmers
Distorts world trade	Subsidy ceiling for richer farmers
Disincentive for Third World farmers	Environmental standards
	Open up to world trade (and especially reduce export subsidies)

A number of reforms were finally adopted in 1988, but none addressed the basic flaws in the CAP. Germany funded a compromise by paying an extra 5 billion ECU[7] to the EC budget over the next five years. Production ceilings were set for all major crops, and price penalties were imposed on producers who exceeded the ceilings. Unfortunately the ceilings were established at relatively high levels, and the fines were low. Member states were also asked to introduce a land set-aside program, as well as early retirement schemes. However, the major problems remained: developments on the world market still did not necessarily influence EC farmers' decisions; the reforms completely ignored the problem of overproductivity; the introduction of environmental standards was not achieved; and the income gap between the highly productive minority of large agricultural producers and the economically less efficient but socially important majority of small-business farmers continued to widen.

More radical steps were needed, and these came with the 1992 MacSharry Reform Package, named after the Irish Agricultural Commissioner Ray MacSharry. By the 1990s, with the proposal of a single currency and the development of the Single Market taking center stage in European politics, the CAP, to some degree, had lost its meaning as one of the vital cornerstones of European integration. Market intervention as practiced in the CAP was an anachronism for a community that advocated the free movement of goods, services, capital, and labor. By the 1990s, moreover, the contribution of the agricultural sector to the GDP and to overall employment had dropped significantly since the 1950s.[8]

MacSharry was appalled by the levels of overproduction still afflicting European agriculture.[9] He attempted to solve this problem by implementing a widespread reduction in prices,[10] land set-aside programs,[11] environmental measures,[12] and direct payments to all producers, large and small, at an average of 207 ECU per hectare.[13]

The result was a massive increase in the cost of the CAP, a consequence of the direct payments and the land set-aside subsidies. MacSharry argued, however, that in the long run the reduced use of agricultural land would lead to significant

Table 12.5. Share of the Agricultural Sector's Workforce (in percent)

	1955*	2004
Austria		5.0
Belgium	9.3	2.2
Bulgaria		10.7
Cyprus		5.1
Czech Republic	4.4	
Denmark	25.4	3.3
Estonia		5.5
Finland		5.0
France	25.9	4.0
Germany	18.9	2.4
Greece		12.6
Hungary		5.3
Ireland	38.8	6.4
Italy	39.5	4.2
Luxembourg	25.0	2.1
Latvia		13.3
Lithuania		16.3
Malta		2.3
Netherlands	13.7	3.0
Poland		17.6
Portugal		12.1
Romania		32.6
Slovakia		5.1
Slovenia		9.7
Spain		5.5
Sweden		2.5
United Kingdom	4.8	1.4

*The 1955 date applies only to the original six member states.
Source: European Commission, DG Agriculture.

savings. More important, the new CAP represented a major shift from a policy of nontransparent consumer subsidies (through higher prices in supermarkets) to one of transparent taxpayer subsidies (through direct payments to farmers). Thus the CAP was now more open to regular public scrutiny and evaluation. MacSharry's reforms also enabled the EU to come to an agreement in the General Agreement on Tariffs and Trade (GATT) rounds. After an agricultural Cold War between the U.S. and the EU that stalled negotiations for seven years, the Uruguay Round finally came to an end in December 1993. The new GATT covered all farm products and further reduced the EU's subsidies to its farmers.[14] Although the GATT certainly did not force the EU to open its agricultural markets to the world, and particularly

Table 12.6. Key Attempts to Reform the CAP

- Stabilizer Reform Package (1988)
- MacSharry Reform Package (1992)
- Agenda 2000 (1997)
- 2003 Reform of the CAP (enlargement, WTO, and Cross Compliance)

to developing countries, it nonetheless represented a much-needed step in the right direction.

The reforms of the early 1990s, however, could not guarantee a stable CAP in the face of continued technical progress and rising productivity. EU members were well aware that drastic reforms were needed to avoid a further budget crisis and to maintain Europe's political legitimacy before increasingly dissatisfied taxpayers. More important, with the countries of Central and Eastern Europe applying for EU membership, a radical overhaul of the CAP seemed appropriate. The Commission argued that the entry of the candidate countries would at least double the agricultural land and the number of people working in agriculture, as well as burden the CAP with an additional 15 billion Euros, an increase of 40 percent.

Responding to this challenge, the Commission, in 1997, published its *Agenda 2000*, proposing reforms that continued down the path taken by MacSharry with a further reduction in prices,[15] along with higher standards for food safety and the environment. The Commission intended to establish a program that would create alternative sources of income for farmers, with the clear aim of reducing the number of CAP recipients. In any case, the Commission estimated that the total costs for the CAP would rise by 6 billion Euros per year. Not surprisingly, the *Agenda 2000* was therefore hotly debated at the Berlin summit in March 1999. French President Jacques Chirac, who had always been responsive to his own domestic agricultural lobby, managed to convince the fourteen other heads of government that enlargement to Central and Eastern Europe remained a remote prospect and therefore immediate action was not required. Hence reform of the CAP, specifically a more widespread cut in prices, was delayed until negotiations with the candidate countries had reached a more mature state—a decision that many commentators judged to be short-sighted. As a minor concession, the new CAP included long overdue standards for food safety and the environment.[16] The summit also agreed to increase direct aid payments, either per hectare or per head of cattle. This meant that at least the annual budget pretty much stayed at the same level of 42.3 billion Euros. The package also meant that further drastic reforms were needed to prepare the CAP for enlargement. The summit acknowledged this by asking the Commission to return with another proposal in 2002. Government leaders found it difficult to confront their agricultural constituencies with the bitter truth that they ought to get used to a future of reduced subsidies and lower guaranteed prices. In the end, the Berlin summit reached a compromise that failed in its attempt to please taxpayers and finance ministers, on one side, and the powerful agricultural lobby, on the other.

A further point of controversy was the reform of the World Trade Organization (WTO). The Seattle meeting in 1999 dramatically displayed the ideological
differences between countries concerning the global market. Many EU trading
partners—particularly the U.S. and Australia—demanded the complete elimination of export subsidies. In return, the EU pointed to other, less transparent forms
of subsidies such as tax breaks, which the U.S. delegation tried not to mention. The
EU also wanted full recognition of the multifunctional role of agriculture, with such
objectives as environmental preservation, landscape conservation, and food safety.
In Seattle, the Agriculture Commissioner Franz Fischler and the Trade Commissioner Pascal Lamy at least offered special trade concessions, such as tariff-free access for the least developed states. Nonetheless, negotiations stalled at the follow-up
meetings in Doha (2001) and in Cancun (2002). Fischler managed to reignite the
debate in December 2002, with a detailed proposal for the next WTO round.[17] The
centerpiece of his plan was to allow goods from the poorest countries to enter the
industrialized world duty free. However, Fischler continued to insist on the socio-
cultural and environmental objectives of the European agricultural model, arguing
that measures supporting such standards ought to be exempt from the reduction
commitments. He also took a parting shot at the United States by pointing out the
need to address export credit systems and shipping food aid merely to dump surpluses in order to keep up prices. The proposal undoubtedly was a step in the right
direction, but the establishment of these unquestionably more favorable conditions
for developing countries depended largely on the ability of First World competitors
to settle their differences.

Regarding enlargement to the countries of Central and Eastern Europe, the
Commission dutifully presented two key proposals on how to rejuvenate the CAP.
In January 2002, DG Agriculture outlined its plans on how to integrate twelve new
member states, which would increase the number of farmers in the EU by 70 percent. The key was the gradual introduction of direct payments, but, in reality, this
meant that, in 2004, farmers in the accession countries would receive only 25 percent
of the financial aid given to their counterparts in Western Europe, with the amount
gradually rising to 100 percent by 2013.[18] Fischler argued that a full introduction of
EU payments would reduce the incentive for badly needed structural reforms in the
farming sectors of Central and Eastern Europe. Clearly the EU did not want to create
a dependency culture, but it had to face the criticism that it was trying to establish a
two-tier system, with accession farmers treated as second-class citizens.

To the Commission's delight, the European summit in Copenhagen in December 2002 fully accepted Fischler's ideas, which then became the legal basis for
organizing agriculture in the post-accession era. The summit also determined the
exact amount of money the new member states could expect, rising from 9.9 billion
Euros in 2004 to 14.9 billion Euros in 2006. This meant that Poland—the largest of
the accession countries—would secure a transfer of 1 billion Euros from the EU's
Structural Funds, and for all new entrants the financial package increased by 408
million Euros. In the end, the costs related to enlargement rose to a total of around

Table 12.7. Enlargement Expenditure, 2004–2006

	2004	2005	2006
Agriculture	1.897	3.737	4.147
Cohesion	6.095	6.940	8.812
Internal policies, transitional expenditure (e.g., nuclear safety)	1.421	1.376	1.351
Administration	503.000	558.000	612.000
Total	9.952	12.657	14.958

37 billion Euros during the 2004–2006 period. The existing member states therefore avoided an increase in their contributions to the EU budget, which currently runs at a maximum of 1.045 percent of their GNP. Instead, enlargement was financed from existing funds.[19]

Fischler's intention to shake up the CAP did not stop with enlargement or the WTO. In July 2002 he proposed further radical steps for the internal reform of the CAP, with a plan that de-coupled subsidies from the amount that farmers produced. The Commission also proposed a new system, "cross compliance," which set conditions for the granting of subsidies: farmers had to follow highly specific guidelines for upholding environmental, animal welfare, and hygienic standards, and for preserving the countryside. Hence Fischler's objective was to address, once and for all, the embarrassing anachronism of the traditional price support scheme that allowed 20 percent of EU farmers to receive 80 percent of CAP money.[20] The member states approved the Commission's idea and this new regime was implemented by mid-2003, with a more detailed list of compliance factors agreed upon at the European Council meeting in June 2005.[21]

As the next step in the EU's long attempt to change its most costly budget item, the so called revision clause called upon the Commission to outline further reform ideas before the end of 2009. If unanimously agreed upon by the European Council, the union might even consider taking some of the proposals onboard before the budget of 2007–13 runs out. But to gain financial room for maneuver, it will be France in particular that is expected to give up some of its current level of subsidies which runs at over 9 billion Euros per year. It remains to be seen whether President Chirac's successor, Nicolas Sarkozy, will be willing and able to convince the influential French agricultural lobby of such a move.

Why Is the CAP So Difficult to Reform?

Given the costs of supporting agriculture in the EU, as well as the high level of bureaucracy and the limited economic contribution that agriculture makes to the Union's prosperity, were all the reforms radical enough? Some analysts believe that the CAP should be abolished,[22] but politics can never be as straightforward as this.

The political reality is that a number of factors continue to guarantee the existence of some form of supranational support for agriculture. First, it is difficult to turn proposals into political action because of the requirement of unanimity voting in the Council of Agricultural Ministers under the consultation procedure. Most often political compromises result in watered down versions of the original proposals. Second, the agricultural sector, although small, continues to have disproportionately powerful influence on domestic politics. Despite the decreasing workforce and agricultural share of the overall GDP, almost no member state government can ignore agricultural welfare. Third, the clash of interests, as set out in the objectives of the CAP in the Treaty of Rome, has never been properly addressed. What's at stake? Agricultural welfare or low consumer prices? So far the EU has tried to maintain an acceptable standard of living for an ever decreasing number of farmers, with consumers and taxpayers footing the bill. A proper equilibrium satisfactory to both sides is almost impossible to obtain. Fourth, the agricultural sector is very well organized both at the national and European levels, and the umbrella pressure group COPA (Committee of Professional Agricultural Organization)[23] is a particularly powerful and determined player in EU politics. Finally, the reality is that the CAP has now been in existence for more than fifty years, and at least two generations of farmers have become accustomed to subsidies. To break this dependency is indeed a formidable task.

13

Economic and Monetary Union

The introduction of a single European currency and the coordination of economic and monetary policies are perhaps the most ambitious aspects of European integration. Without historical precedent, the launch of the Euro in 1999 was awaited with much euphoria, but also some skepticism. This chapter establishes the reasons for launching EMU and points up the criteria that member states must now meet in managing their national economies. The discussion then turns to an analysis of the advantages of having a supranational EMU while also focusing on the potential and real shortcomings. The key issues are the following:

1. What are the economic and political benefits and costs of EMU?
2. Why did the member states embark on an EMU?
3. What are the implications of a more or less independent European Central Bank?

Political-Economic Challenges

Economic and Monetary Union is a classic example of political economy and how public authorities manage a state's economic and social well-being through political, economic and fiscal policies. Of the many approaches to political economy, the theories of John Maynard Keynes have long been the most influential in driving Western governments to adopt proactive, economic policies moderating the societal effects of alternating recessions and economic booms. Keynesianism was adopted successfully in the United States by President Franklin D. Roosevelt in the 1930s, at the height of the Great Depression. During this world economic crisis, the Roosevelt administration undertook massive public works projects to create jobs.[1] Roosevelt calculated that a growth in employment could boost the economy, since people simply would have more money to buy products. According to Keynes, the money required for such massive public projects would eventually be recuperated by increased tax revenues arising from the subsequent economic upturn. He referred to this investment by the state as deficit spending and argued that governments should adopt a so-called anti-cyclical policy, meaning that in a time of recession state authorities should act as if the overall economic climate was positive.[2]

Keynesian principles were questioned in the 1970s as a result of a steep increase in oil prices, a devalued U.S. dollar, and widespread recession across many Western countries. One of Keynes's chief critics, Milton Friedman of the University of Chicago, argued the opposite of Keynes. Instead of being a proactive actor, the state should not intercede in the economy but should retreat and concentrate only on providing a stable monetary framework within which market forces could freely interact. This so-called monetarist theory is based on the principle that governments should never act to moderate business cycles but should concentrate on stabilizing the value and supply of money.[3]

Governments have various instruments with which to fine-tune and manage their economies. To name just two, interest rates can be regulated[4] as can minimum bank reserves.[5] Apart from these monetary instruments, a government's tax policy—directly through income taxes or indirectly through sales taxes and on duties imposed on tobacco, petrol or alcohol—can also be effective, as it directly affects consumers' disposable income. Every government is also an employer, and so setting wages naturally has an impact on the amount of money that can be spent on cinema tickets, restaurants, and holidays.

The key economic objectives that governments must attempt to meet are growth, high employment levels, and price stability and trade balance. Governments often find it difficult, however, to keep all four objectives in balance. For example, if a positive investment climate increases employment and therefore economic growth, inflation may result as prices often rise when businesses attempt to profit from higher disposable income. Inflationary tendencies, in turn, may lead to a negative trade balance, as exports become more expensive. The end result may be reduced employment as companies lay off staff, which then would lead to a decline in economic growth.

Clearly, therefore, societies that attempt to reform their monetary and economic systems face potentially monumental changes. This chapter describes how EU member states approached this delicate balancing act by focusing on the instruments, provisions, and institutions that now determine monetary and economic matters in the EU. The process was quite daunting: to merge different national policies for managing their economies into a unified and coherent European standard.

What Is an Economic and Monetary Union?

EMU refers, above all, to the establishment of a single European currency—the Euro—which eliminates exchange-rate controls for financial transactions, and allows businesses and consumers to freely trade across borders without paying to convert money from one currency to another. EMU also includes a common pool of foreign exchange reserves and a single standard group of monetary instruments, such as a single interest rate and one minimum reserve set by a European Central Bank (ECB).

Some analysts believe that only a single currency would truly complete the EU's Single Market; otherwise different interest rates would result in different prices across Europe. Price differences would undermine the free movement of capital, as money would end up in the countries offering the best rates, as well as the free movement of goods, which would be bought in countries where prices were lowest. Moreover, federalists saw in EMU a way to accelerate the move toward political integration, as Europe's economic challenges could only be met by a single decision maker with state-like authority. In the run-up to the Maastricht negotiations in 1991, EMU was also regarded as a means for integrating an ever more economically powerful and unified Germany.[6]

The Road to EMU

Article 2 of the Treaty of Rome (1957) had already promulgated the "progressive approximation of the economic policies of member states." Although the treaty had no provisions for creating a regional currency bloc, a bloc was not seen as necessary since the Bretton Woods system of 1945 established fixed exchange rates using the U.S. dollar as the undisputed global monetary standard. Monetary integration was not on the agenda in the 1950s, at which time European economic integration was more concerned with trade, particularly trade in goods. The Werner Report of 1970, however, changed this perspective. In the previous year U.S. President Richard Nixon had abandoned Bretton Woods, a move that led to a much cheaper dollar; The Hague Summit of 1969 reacted by giving the task of exploring monetary integration to a committee chaired by Luxembourg Prime Minister Pierre

Werner and comprised of bankers from several central banks across Europe as well as leading officials from the European Commission. The committee produced a three-stage plan to achieve EMU: fix exchange rates; complete the free circulation of goods, services, capital, and persons; and centralize monetary policies. The report also recommended the creation of a community system of central banks and a new organization for deciding economic policies. The report caused severe disagreement over the strategy of how EMU might be achieved, a detail Werner had not specified. Belgium and France argued for the implementation of a single currency to generate economic convergence, whereas Germany and the Netherlands advocated the opposite—first convergence and then a single currency. In the end, EMU was buried by the oil shock of 1973 and the subsequent recession across Western Europe.

Another idea that emerged in 1972, termed the "Snake," allowed European currencies to fluctuate in a narrow band of plus or minus 2.25 percent of the U.S. dollar. But the international exchange-rate market was so volatile that the British pound, the Irish punt, the Italian lira, the Danish crown, and the French franc were forced to abandon the Snake soon after. The problem was straightforward: the economies of Europe at that stage were simply too divergent. On one side was the Deutschmark with low interest and inflation rates and on the other were countries like Italy, France, and the UK with high interest and inflation rates, which subjected their currencies to speculation and overvaluation.

Not until 1979 was a more coherent system established. The brainchild of German Chancellor Helmut Schmidt and French President Valerie Giscard d'Estaing, the European Monetary System (EMS) created a zone of relative monetary stability and was promptly supported by Denmark, the Netherlands, Belgium, and Luxembourg, with Ireland, the U.K., and Italy adopting a wait-and-see approach. Similar to the Snake, it proposed a 2.25 percent margin,[7] but this time it was not pinned to the U.S. dollar but to bilateral relationships between the currencies involved. Also in contrast to the Snake, national central banks were required to intervene when a currency approached the upper or lower limit of 2.25 percent. Of overall importance, the EMS established the European Currency Unit (ECU), a basket of all European currencies used as a means of settlement between European central banks (see Table 13.1).[8]

By the early 1990s, however, the EMS came under intense pressure. The immense costs of German unification raised the country's public debt to new heights and prompted a weakening of the Deutschmark and a subsequent loss in market confidence in the ECU. Speculation began to accelerate with currencies that were seen as candidates for devaluation such as the lira, the French franc, and the British pound. Fueled by massive speculation by, for instance, the financier George Soros, the U.K. was forced to abandon the EMS on September 16, 1992.[9] Later, the currency-fluctuation margins were increased to plus or minus 15 percent, which was merely a verbal token to monetary convergence.

Table 13.1. The European Monetary System and the European Currency Unit (ECU)

Member State currency	Percentage of ECU value 1979	Percentage of ECU value 1989
Germany	33.0	30.53
France	19.8	20.79
Netherlands	10.5	10.21
Belgium/Luxembourg	9.5	8.91
Italy	9.5	7.21
Denmark	3.0	2.71
Ireland	1.1	1.08
United Kingdom	13.6	11.17
Greece	—	0.49
Spain	—	4.24
Portugal	—	0.71

The Final Steps toward EMU

The EMS crisis of 1992 could not stop EMU. Already in 1988, the Delors Report had described in detail a three-stage plan that would be used as a blueprint for establishing EMU.

- Stage 1: the completion of the Single Market, particularly free capital movement and macroeconomic coordination, by July 1990
- Stage 2: coordination between national central banks within a system comprised of European central banks
- Stage 3: fixed exchange rates, resulting in a single monetary policy and currency, and the establishment of a European Central Bank

EMU, and with it the merging of national currencies, required new tools for developing, coordinating, and managing economic and monetary policies. To accomplish this, the European Council created two institutions to ensure a smooth implementation of EMU: the European Central Bank (ECB),[10] which acts independently of political authorities and is authorized to issue money solely to maintain price stability, and a European System of Central Banks (ESCB), comprised of national central bank officials and the ECB, and responsible for conducting foreign-exchange operations. Finally, a more central role was given to ECOFIN (the meeting of national economies and finance ministers within the Council of Ministers), so that it could produce broad guidelines for economic policies within the EU.

Delors also learned from the Werner Commission's mistake of not providing guidelines for implementing its recommendations. The Stability and Growth Pact, adopted in 1997, issued clear guidelines on how convergence could be achieved: member states wishing to participate in EMU agreed to satisfy convergence criteria that

Table 13.2. EMU's Convergence Criteria

1. Price stability (inflation rate of no more than 1.5 percent above the three best performing states)
2. Limited public debt (no more than 3 percent of GDP annually and a total of no more than 60 percent of GDP)
3. Limited exchange rate fluctuation (remain within EMS for two years)
4. Reasonably low interest rates (no more than 2 percent above the three best performers)

shaped national economic and monetary policies, not only in the run-up to EMU but also as long as the Stability and Growth Pact remained in place (Table 13.2).

Although Delors had provided the EU with a clear timetable from which there was no turning back, EMU was a typical European compromise: Germany achieved its objective of having the ECB organized along the lines of its own national central bank and functioning as a watchdog on inflation, but France managed to push the other member states into a clear commitment toward an ever closer union.

Not every member state was enthusiastic about Delors's plan. During previous negotiations over the Maastricht Treaty, the UK and Denmark had secured an opt-out and decided to stay outside EMU.[11] Sweden, which joined the EU after the Maastricht Treaty in 1995, also decided against the Euro in a referendum in 2004. In the end, eleven countries embarked on the project in 1999,[12] with Greece joining in 2001 after managing to reduce its public debt to acceptable levels. As for countries that joined the EU in 2004, their eventual participation in EMU was one of the vital entry criteria. But every accession state had a different timetable that was set by the European Commission in line with the country's economic performance and structure. Slovenia, as the first new member, introduced the Euro in January 2007, followed by Malta and Cyprus in January 2008.

The Pros and Cons of EMU

A number of factors undoubtedly make a convincing case for the introduction of the Euro and EMU. Without the need to exchange money from one currency to another, businesses and consumers save approximately 2 percent on transaction costs, and importers and exporters within EMU no longer face the risk of currency fluctuations.[13] Another factor is that the transnational coordination offered by the ESCB makes it unlikely that Europe will see a repetition of the 1992 crisis that forced the British pound out of the European Monetary System. Although the EU has often been criticized as distant, bureaucratic, and faceless with no distinct tangible identity, the Euro now gives Europeans a concrete reminder of their existence within a community of European states. Daily, and even more often when traveling to other countries of the Eurozone, simply by paying with notes and coins, Europeans become aware that they form part of an entity that goes beyond their national environment.

But despite these positive experiences, a number of shortcomings still offer plenty of ammunition to critics of the Euro. The most notable problem has been the rise in prices across the Eurozone, which surprised both economists and consumers. The increases were sometimes so steep that even German Chancellor Gerhard Schröder and Italian Prime Minister Silvio Berlusconi publicly pleaded with businesses to stop their profiteering practices. Ironically many businesses, mostly restaurants, were able to get away with hefty price rises, because their customers found it difficult to manage the mental conversion from their national currency into Euros.[14]

The single European currency also has split the instruments for managing an economy between the supranational level, where the ECB sets interest rates and the minimum reserve for the whole Eurozone, and the national level, where governments still control fiscal policies and are involved in some wage bargaining processes. This arrangement potentially could result in a scenario where a national government, having lost control over interest rates and minimum reserves, is forced to counterbalance the effects of the ECB's interest rate rise by raising taxes and lowering wages.[15]

Also coming under severe criticism was the Stability Pact of the Maastricht Treaty, which is the basis of EMU. Romano Prodi, Commission President from 1999 to 2004, described the pact as the "Stupidity Pact," given the rigid criteria with which member states had to comply. Particularly disquieting was the requirement to have a maximum annual deficit of 3 percent of GDP.[16] Underlying this criterion was the straightforward idea that countries wishing to adopt the single currency should have a balanced budget, thus sheltering the Euro against inflationary pressures. But critics of the pact argue that this is too rigid a criterion and curtails a country's ability to proactively shape its economy and provide investment boosts in times of economic slowdown. A solution would be to adhere to the deficit level of 3 percent but increase the time span during which it is applied. A country could then go into debt, for instance, 4 percent one year, as long as the average deficit over five years does not exceed the level agreed upon. However, the Stability Pact is part of the Maastricht Treaty, and any treaty revision requires the consent of all member states. For now, the controversy over the Reform Treaty and the envisaged integration of Turkey has moved this issue to the bottom of the political agenda.

Given that the Euro has only been in place since January 1999, judgment on a number of other issues might be premature, and it will be some time before signs emerge of any positive or negative implications. Among these issues, Euroskeptics often question whether a single currency is truly required for a single market. Yes, when buying a car, consumers can use the Internet to easily identify the country offering the cheapest deal. For bigger and more expensive items, transnational price comparisons are indeed done on an increasingly regular basis. But would consumers fly to Vienna only because the Austrian MacDonald's offers the cheapest Big Mac in Europe? We have already seen an approximation of prices in the Eurozone,

Table 13.3. Advantages and Disadvantages of EMU

Advantages

1. Lowers transaction costs
2. Does away with exchange rate uncertainty, leading to a more predictable investment climate
3. Transnational coordination makes a repetition of the 1992 crisis unlikely
4. Concrete symbol for a European identity

Disadvantages

1. Divides the instruments for managing the economy between member states and the ECB
2. Reduces the number of tools for member states to combat national economic problems
3. Stringent convergence criteria (particularly an annual budget deficit of 3 percent of the GDP) mean less flexibility for member states
4. Creates a three-tier Europe: those who are in, those who are out but want to be in, and those who want to stay out

Verdict Still Out

1. Is a single currency truly required for a Single Market?
2. Is one currency appropriate for a region with hugely dissimilar economic structures?
3. Can the ECB and ECOFIN coordinate their policies?
4. To what extent can the ECB maiantain its independence?

especially in big metropolitan areas, and price differences probably will remain largely as a result of the still significant variations in national tax rates.

Some analysts also point to the danger of having a single currency for a region with such highly dissimilar economic structures. When comparing the highly developed economies of northern Europe with those of the south, particularly Spain, Portugal, and Greece, one has reason to believe that a single currency and a common monetary approach might not be the best solution to guarantee growth and prosperity for all. The stringent convergence criteria of the Stability Pact also mean that large-scale public investment to help economically backward countries improve their competitiveness is hardly possible.[17] We are already witnessing a dilemma, where a single interest rate is not suitable for the whole of the Eurozone: Ireland, for instance, needs a higher rate, but Portugal needs a lower rate to improve its investment climate. The argument thus put forward is that the EU is not an Optimum Currency Area (OCA).

On the other hand, there are several countries with their own national currencies that do not represent an OCA. In Britain, London and the booming southeast stand in marked contrast to the country's laggard northern regions. In the U.S., Arizona and Florida have much higher growth rates than the rust belt states of Michigan and Pennsylvania. Again, time and continued practice will tell how governments will adapt to a unified European monetary approach, and how they will use their remaining tools for economic management to positive effect. Attracting foreign investment, for example, is not only a function of interest rates; the case of Ireland has shown that an educated workforce, tax incentives, and a conducive business climate can also result in a great boost to a country's economic performance.

A further point of concern about the single currency is the coordination of policies between the ECB and ECOFIN. The objective of the former is simply to maintain price stability. Unlike the U.S. Federal Reserve, which sets interest rates by analyzing the country's overall economic performance, the ECB's sole mandate is to keep inflation under control. ECOFIN, however, analyzes the larger economic parameters of the Eurozone, decides when intervention in foreign exchange markets is required, and offers broad guidelines for the fiscal policies of member states. It also has the right to impose fines when member states violate the Stability Pact. The objective of the ECB is clear-cut, but the same cannot be said of ECOFIN. Tax policies are still set and decided upon at the national level, which means that ECOFIN's guidelines have no force of law. Moreover, to avoid friction between European partners, so far it has not issued fines for violations of the Stability Pact. Up to now, no one can say that the two organizations are working hand in hand, and though the Eurozone undoubtedly has a monetary government (the ECB), ECOFIN still falls short of being described as a unified economic government.

Questions have also arisen over whether the ECB can maintain its independence from any political influence. In line with its own domestic version, Germany insisted that the Bank should be immune to political pressure; indeed, over the past ten years, the ECB has ignored calls from politicians arguing for changing rates. The problem is that although the somewhat sluggish growth in the Eurozone since 1999 has prompted many member-state ministers to plead with the ECB to lower rates, neither the first ECB president Wim Duisenberg (1994–2002) nor his successor Jean Claude Trichet have moved an inch away from their sole objective of keeping inflation under control.

14

Justice and Home Affairs

The Maastricht Treaty added a further dimension to the construction of Europe: Justice and Home Affairs (JHA), which brings together the member states' ministries of justice and the interior. JHA allows for dialogue and cooperation between police, customs and immigration services, and justice departments. The areas JHA covers are vast and include all internal security issues. Among the most significant are matters related to EU citizenship, asylum, immigration, and police and judicial cooperation. Those areas are examined in this chapter by addressing the following questions:

1. Why do member states cooperate in JHA?
2. How meaningful is the concept of EU citizenship?
3. How unified are asylum and immigration policies across the EU?
4. How has the EU responded to the events of 9/11?

Reasons for Establishing JHA

Arguably the main achievement of the EU was the establishment of a Single Market founded on the free movement of goods, services, capital, and people. The Schengen agreement, which came into force in 1985, removed internal border controls between participating countries and helped to further cement this privilege. While the Single Market and Schengen undoubtedly gave many benefits to European citizens, there was a downside to the ability to move freely across the continent. Terrorists, drug and human traffickers, money launderers, and organized crime could take advantage of a more open Europe. In the end, one member state's security problem could become a security challenge for others. Improvements in police and judicial cooperation, therefore, have often been seen as a functional spillover of the Single Market program and the single currency.

Greater integration in these fields was also needed following a number of political developments beginning with the social and political upheavals following the end of Communism in Eastern Europe and the Balkans. By the mid-1990s, new transit routes through the former Communist countries had been established and greatly facilitated the flow of drugs. Illegal trafficking of humans was also on the rise, as was the establishment of transnational mafia networks. Military conflicts following the breakup of Yugoslavia resulted in significant waves of refugees entering Western Europe and exacerbated the new security challenges confronting the EU. Adding to the challenges, the terrorist attacks on the United States on September 11, 2001, greatly accelerated political decisions at the EU level. During that time, public concern over illegal immigration and the subsequent success of several right-wing parties also encouraged member states to advance co-operation in the JHA field.

JHA Prior to Maastricht

In the 1970s the terrorism problem in Western Europe had already worsened sharply. The Irish Republican Army in Northern Ireland, the Baader-Meinhof gang in West Germany, and the Red Brigades in Italy shocked the political establishment. The hostage taking and murders of the Israeli team at the Munich Olympics in 1972 revealed that Europe was not immune to the political upheavals in the Middle East. To meet these threats, the Trevi Group[1] of interior and justice ministers began to meet regularly starting in 1976. These Trevi meetings were conducted ad hoc, outside the EU framework, and strictly among national governments. Also, the Trevi Group did not set up any institutions or policy structures but concentrated purely on the exchange of information and communication on how best to combat transnational crimes.

JHA in the 1990s: From Maastricht to Amsterdam

The dramatically changing international political climate of the 1990s, including the emerging security vacuum in Central and Eastern Europe and the conflicts in the former Yugoslavia demanded a swift response from the EU. At Maastricht, in addition to setting up a second pillar focusing on the Common Foreign and Security Policy, the EU also established Pillar III called Justice and Home Affairs. Within this pillar, the member states agreed on areas of common interest including asylum, external borders, immigration, drug addiction, and judicial cooperation on civil and criminal matters, customs, and the policing of drug trafficking, organized crime, and terrorism.

But despite the ever growing security challenges, concerns over sovereignty remained and slowed progress in this area. When the Amsterdam Treaty was signed in 1997, the member states finally agreed to establish an "area of freedom, security, and justice" in the EU. As a first step, Amsterdam integrated the Schengen Agreement; it then moved policy making on visas, asylum, and immigration from Pillar III to Pillar I, giving Community institutions a greater role in the policy-making process. Limitations to this shift of sovereignty remained, however, as the role of the Commission, the European Parliament, and the European Court of Justice continued to be more restricted than in other policy areas of Pillar I. What was left in the third pillar was police and judicial cooperation in criminal matters.[2] Although the Amsterdam Treaty represented a distinct move toward more supranational decision making in matters relating to internal security, little progress was made in arriving at a common approach to asylum and to visas and immigration, where different standards prevailed across the EU.[3]

Citizenship

EU citizenship, as with any relationship between a government and its citizens, entails rights, duties, and involvement in political life, with the purpose of creating a European public domain and some form of a European political identity (see Table 14.1). Access to EU citizenship is granted through the member states; one must first gain citizenship in one of the member states, which then automatically grants that person EU citizenship.[4] Thus EU citizenship is not regulated by EU laws but is determined by differing national regulations. For instance, the children of an immigrant from Turkey might receive German citizenship, and thus the rights of EU citizenship, only after a naturalization process that could take ten years or more, as Germany has traditionally relied on the principle of *jus sanguinis* (the law of kinship), which grants citizenship in line with that of one's parents. But if the Turkish immigrant had chosen Ireland as his destination and would start and raise a family there, his children would automatically be granted Irish and EU citizenship, as Ireland broadly follows the principle of *jus soli* (law of the land), which grants citizenship based on one's birthplace.

The differences in national laws, therefore, have resulted in a patchwork of EU citizenship across Europe. An example is the right to schooling. In the UK, Muslims have the right to be educated according to their faith. But Muslims in Sweden do not have this right, as Sweden does not have a sufficiently large Muslim population to make religious public schooling practical. Although some unifying features did emanate from the Maastricht Treaty, the entire agenda of citizens' rights and responsibilities is largely determined by differing national sets of citizenship.

Table 14.1. EU Citizenship as Defined by the Maastricht Treaty

- Right to move freely and reside on EU territory
- Right to vote and stand in local and EP elections
- Right to diplomatic protection by a member state of one's choice
- Right to petition the EP and ombudsman
- Principle of non-discrimination on the grounds of nationality, gender, race, religion, disability, age, and sexual orientation
- Equal access to the EU's civil service

On the other hand, some positive and notable developments associated with the incorporation of the Schengen Agreement have included a common approach in the EU on how to handle non-EU foreigners. Non-EU visitors can travel freely across the Schengen area for a period of up to three months if they have a valid travel document and sufficient money to cover their living costs. Furthermore, the Schengen countries have integrated their visa rules, and there is now a single list of countries whose citizens require a visa.

Asylum and Immigration

OECD statistics indicate that, before the 2004 enlargement, about 1.5 million legal immigrants entered the EU annually, with about 13 million non-EU nationals living in the old EU-15, comprising about 4 percent of the total EU population. The International Organization for Migration estimated that between 120,000 and 500,000 foreigners enter the EU illegally every year.[5] Asylum seekers constitute a significant number of foreigners entering the EU annually. The right to asylum is governed, in general, by the Geneva Convention of 1951 to which all member states are signatories. The Convention states that "no one may be removed, expelled or extradited to a state where there is a serious risk that he or she would be subjected to death penalty, torture or other inhuman or degrading treatment or punishment." But apart from this general prerogative, the status of immigrants and asylum applicants is still determined by different sets of national regulations and standards. Throughout the 1990s the flow of persons seeking international protection in the EU increased substantially, mainly following the breakup of the former Soviet empire and Yugoslavia, which dramatically necessitated a common solution in line with each member state's capacities for absorbing immigrants.

At the JHA summit in Tampere, Finland, in October 1999, the member states agreed to develop a single EU asylum system, which aimed to create unified procedures and a uniform status for those granted asylum. Member states also asked the Commission to produce more specific proposals on the precise nature of a common approach to asylum and immigration. A response came in November 2000, when the Commission issued a "road map" for an EU-wide policy that called on member states to both secure the rights of long-term foreign residents and asylum applicants, and combat illegal immigration and trafficking by reinforcing partnerships with the countries of origin. Regarding asylum, the Commission did not propose a new EU agency but agreed to a set of principles governing how each member state would assess asylum cases.[6]

The Tampere summit differentiated two phases: the first, ending in 2004, would lay the foundation for integrating border controls and requiring police and judicial cooperation in the recognition of judicial decisions; the second, based on the initial ground work, would guarantee fundamental rights, access to justice for third country nationals, and protection under the Geneva Convention, as well as regulate migration, control external borders, and combat organized cross-border crime and threats of terrorism. Over the past few years EU leaders managed to agree on a limited number of legislative proposals in this area.[7] Important stepping stones included the 1995 resolution on minimum guarantees for asylum procedures, the 1997 Amsterdam Treaty that established a common European asylum system, the 2002 agreement regarding a common definition for persons eligible for refugee and subsidiary protection status, and the September 2003 directive on family reunification.

A key innovation resulting from the Tampere summit was the European Refugee Fund (ERF) established in 2000. Jointly funded by member states, the ERF allocates financial aid to member states to balance the burdens borne by providing for asylum and displaced refugees. The fund also supports special projects for the reception, integration, and repatriation of refugees and displaced persons. Despite its modest budget, financially it is the largest EU program on asylum and immigration. For the period 2000–2004, when its first funding cycle came to an end, the ERF had disbursed a total of 216 million Euros. On 12 February 2004 the European Commission adopted a proposal to extend the ERF for the period 2005–2010 and tripled the size of the fund to accommodate the ten new member states. The proposal also boosted financial and technical assistance to third countries in the area of migration management and created a new program for the period 2004–2008 at a total cost of 250 million Euros.

At a summit meeting in The Hague in November 2004, EU leaders emphasized that the EU's common asylum policy should be based on a fair sharing of responsibility and costs, and on closer cooperation between member states. In an ambitious move, the summit also envisaged a uniform status for people granted asylum, joint processing of asylum applications outside EU territory, and a single assessment procedure. At a subsequent meeting in The Hague in May 2005, member states agreed to change the governance rules that would thereafter apply to EU policy making in this area. The changes included a move to qualified majority voting, co-decision powers for the European Parliament, and an enhanced role for the European Court of Justice in asylum and immigration matters, except for economic migration.

In 2005 another remarkable step was the establishment of FRONTEX (with the cumbersome official name of European Agency for the Management of Operational

Cooperation at the External Borders).[8] Even candidate and accession countries started to tackle migration in a structurally more coherent manner; MARRI (the Migration, Asylum, Refugees Regional Initiative) was formed in 2004 and included as its members Albania, Bosnia-Herzegovina, Croatia, Macedonia, Serbia, and Montenegro.[9]

Clearly asylum and immigration have become top priorities for the EU. The JHA Council held as many as eight meetings per year, and summit meetings devoted to the subject, took place, such as in Tampere in 1999 and Seville in 2002, demonstrating the political urgency of these matters. Considering that member states remained reluctant to transfer powers over their borders, the amount of authority that they did transfer to the EU was remarkable. This was largely owing to the recognition that unilateral responses in this policy area were often ineffective in an increasingly interdependent world and the realization that intergovernmental decision-making procedures were often too slow and therefore incapable of providing effective policy solutions.

Judicial and Police Cooperation

Judicial cooperation in civil matters concerns, for example, problems that arise over the mutual recognition by different member states of court judgments in divorce or child custody cases or commercial questions such as bankruptcy, where two or more member states are involved. The EU has adopted legislation on the mutual recognition of court judgments relating to divorce and parental responsibility, as well as for settling cross-border disputes involving civil claims. Judicial cooperation in criminal matters concerns, for instance, extradition and other cross-border crimes such as drug and human trafficking, terrorism, or crimes concerned with computer security. Further legislative proposals ensure that court orders in one member state—for instance, imposing fines or confiscating assets—are implemented throughout the EU. Also noteworthy is the establishment of the European arrest warrant that came into force in January 2004 and resolved the problem of cumbersome and often lengthy extradition procedures between member states.

Again, the European Council meeting in Tampere in October 1999 represented a breakthrough for cooperation between the judiciary and police. The summit proposed the harmonization of criminal law in some areas, and also created a host of new agencies to help police authorities. The most important one, the European Police Office or Europol, had already been agreed upon in 1995 but was not fully functional until 1999.[10] The Tampere summit also created a European judicial unit (Eurojust, based in The Hague) comprised of a high-level network of national criminal prosecutors with the task of fostering judicial cooperation. The summit also set up a European Police College (CEPOL) and the Police Chief's Task Force, which brings together senior officials for frequent meetings.[11] Despite this impressive number of institutions, progress in the field of police and judicial cooperation has remained sluggish and dominated by deep divisions between member states, as

Table 14.2. Europol

- Budget: 55 million Euros
- Staff: 400
- Functions:
  - -providing information exchanges
  - -coordinating multinational operations
  - -maintaining transnational databases
  - -preventing Euro counterfeiting

many are reluctant to relinquish authority over one of the most crucial aspects of a country's national sovereignty.[12] Not surprisingly, the 9/11 attacks on the World Trade Center and the Pentagon in the U.S. resulted in a political urgency to equip European countries with mechanisms to counter potential terrorist threats. Although 9/11 did not bring about many completely new policy proposals, it did accelerate the approval of four proposals that had originated two years earlier, around the time of the Tampere summit:

- an anti-terrorism task force within Europol
- a European arrest warrant replacing the traditional method of extradition
- a list of thirty-two extraditable crimes, including terrorism
- a common definition of terrorism and specific minimum sentences for various terrorist offences

Hence there was a remarkable turnaround from the sluggishness of the early 1990s to speedy action after 1999 as a result of the combined external pressure of the terrorist attacks in New York (2001), Madrid (2004), and London (2005), as well as the security problems emanating from Central and Eastern Europe. The ultimate authority over police and judicial cooperation, however, still rests with national governments, although the emerging institutions such as Europol did allow greater cooperation and communication between member states.

The Lisbon Treaty of 2007 would represent a further boost to JHA. Subject to ratification after the negative referendum in Ireland in June 2008, Lisbon introduces qualified majority voting for judicial and police cooperation in criminal matters, and asylum and immigration. In addition, previous restrictions on the European Court of Justice to rule in cases relating to JHA (asylum, visa, illegal immigration, and judicial cooperation in criminal and civilian matters) would also be lifted. The United Kingdom and Denmark, however, continue to favor a national over a European approach in these matters, with the latter opting out completely from the JHA agenda, while Britain continues to decide on a case-by-case basis whether to accept JHA rules. This means that the judicial and political authorities of both countries remain unaffected by ECJ rulings in these areas.

15

Common Foreign and Security Policy

Discussions on foreign and defense policies in the European Union have often been nebulous, more pretence than substance. Crucial questions of whether and how to move beyond national interests toward a truly supranational authority in foreign policy have hardly been considered throughout the fifty-year existence of the EU. The early failings in the 1950s of French Prime Minister Renee Pleven to establish the so-called European Defense Community testified to the political reality that Europe's agenda, up until the 1990s, was dominated by the overwhelming influence of the Cold War, trapping Europe within the global power struggle between the United States and the Soviet Union.

In the end, indecisiveness and conflicting opinions over the precise nature of the European project contributed to shortcomings in the sphere of Common Foreign and Security Policy. Granted, in 1997, the EU established the post of High Representative for CFSP, which was followed up in 2007 with the proposal to create the post of "High Representative of the Union for Foreign Affairs and Security Policy" (which would merge the two previously existing roles of High Representative for CFSP and the External Relations Commissioner). Nonetheless, the bitter debate over Europe's involvement in Iraq in 2003 offered a reminder that the member states still have not reached a convincing consensus over the EU's scope, direction, and aspirations: should it be a federal union with far-reaching supranational political, economic, and social powers or merely a "trading union" whereby supranational integration would be confined to an economic agenda? Because the EU continues to be more than an international organization but less than a coherent polity, it is lackluster in the area of foreign and security policy. In this context, this chapter addresses three main questions:

1. Why have developments in foreign and security policy been so slow compared to, for instance, the Single Market initiatives?
2. Does Europe have a coherent foreign policy?
3. What instruments does the EU employ to pursue its common foreign policy, and what are the Union's geographical spheres of activity?

Security in the Post–Cold War Era

During the Cold War, security was synonymous with the defense of territory, with NATO and the Warsaw Pact as its guarantors. After the breakup of the Communist empire, security acquired a new and complex dimension: nonterritorial threats increasingly dominate the international agenda, including terrorism, drug trafficking, nuclear waste, ethnic conflicts, economic and social imbalances, environmental problems, and human disasters. A new threat has been the emergence of new actors in international politics other than states that act without any reference to national interests (with Al Quaida being the most prominent example). Hence security post-1989 seems to be linked to issues rather than to states (albeit Saddam Hussein's Iraq represents the notable exception).

To face the challenges of this new world order, the United States relies on an enormous military capacity. The U.S. spends more on defense than France, the UK, Germany, Japan, China, Russia, and India combined. The U.S. also is the only country in the world that can intervene at will at any time, anywhere on the globe. U.S. technology enables the country to wage war with limited (American) casualties. This prime military position will continue long into the future, since the U.S. also spends five times more money on military research and development than all of Europe combined.

It is in this context that one must assess the changing role of the North Atlantic Treaty Organization (NATO). The events of 2002 witnessed major changes for the Alliance. In that year a new NATO–Russian Council (NRC) was established to achieve cooperation in missile defense and in the fight against terrorism and nuclear proliferation. The NATO summit in Prague in November 2002 also paved the way for integrating seven more EU members from Central and Eastern Europe.[1] However, fundamental problems persist. NATO remains a large and conservative organization with decision-making procedures still based on consensus, requiring the agreement of all its twenty-six members. In military matters, the alliance continues to rely heavily on the United States. Ironically, though, the U.S. does not necessarily involve NATO in its military operations, as seen in Iraq, where the U.S. forged ahead without NATO. Further questions also remain regarding NATO's future objectives. With Russia now a possible partner, who is the next enemy? And with Europe on the verge of taking on new responsibilities with the establishment of the EU's Rapid Reaction Force (see below), where does NATO fit in the new world order?

An answer to that question was proposed by the former U.S. secretary of defense Donald Rumsfeld at the NATO summit in Prague in 2002, when he convinced the European partners to mount a Rapid Response Force of up to twenty-one thousand troops, to be deployable within five to thirty days and for relatively brief operations against terrorists anywhere in the world. Some commentators judged this move as a cynical attempt by the U.S. to use NATO for its war against Al-Quaida, but the end result, in any case, was a remarkable change in NATO's envisaged function: a transformation from a defense organization into a force capable of preemptive military action. Undoubtedly Rumsfeld bred at least momentary life into the Alliance, with the welcomed side effect of satisfying American national interests. But this could not hide the fact that NATO is an ailing patient, struggling to find a coherent purpose and objective.

Chronology of the Common Foreign and Security Policy

The first attempt to establish a coherent foreign and defense policy at the European level emerged in the ambitious plan by the French prime minister Rene Pleven for a European Defense Community (EDC). The outbreak of the Korean War in 1950 had prompted widespread fears that the Cold War might intensify and that Korea was merely a prelude to a showdown between the world's two ideological camps. Harry S. Truman, U.S. president at the time, made it quite clear to his West European colleagues that he expected Europe to share the burden of global confrontation, particularly to provide for its own security. American demands grew more urgent during the debate over the future of West Germany's military complex. Clearly any defense force could only benefit from the economic and technological might of Western Europe's most populous country. However, the lesson learned from two world wars was that a coherent strategy had to be found to satisfactorily and safely integrate West German forces into the community of Western democratic states. Pleven's EDC offered just that: a European army composed of national contingents, with a supranational foreign minister, in which all participating states, except for West Germany, could maintain command of their own national units. Britain was the first country to veto the plan, favoring instead the looser intergovernmental Western European Union (WEU), which was merely an extension of the 1948 Treaty of Brussels that Italy and West Germany were invited to join in 1954.[2] Nevertheless, despite Britain's refusal to join, the original EU-6 embraced the EDC in 1952, but Pleven's bold plan failed ratification in France where political sentiment was

Table 15.1. Developments in the Common Foreign and Security Policy

1948: Brussels Treaty Organization (later renamed the Western European Union)
1952: Pleven Plan to establish the European Defence Community
1954: French Parliament refuses to ratify the EDC
1969: Hague summit establishes European Political Cooperation
1992: Maastricht Treaty introduces CFSP as Pillar II of the EU
1997: Amsterdam Treaty introduces the position of High Representative
1998: St. Malo Initiative (France, UK) gives Europe the capacity to act autonomously
1999: Helsinki summit agrees to set up a Rapid Response Force by 2003

largely opposed to such ambitious supranational ideals. With hardly an option left, the original six, along with Britain, settled on the WEU. But without armed forces, the WEU was only an administrative and consultative organ that merely added a European perspective to NATO's decisions.

The next proposal to foster foreign policy at a European level came at the summit in The Hague in 1969, and was termed European Political Cooperation (EPC). An initiative by the newly elected French president Georges Pompidou, EPC turned out to be simply an intergovernmental and bilateral forum for foreign ministers and heads of governments. Supported by a network of national officials and committees, and fiercely guarding its independence from the European Community, EPC established the so-called common position as a political means to establish foreign policy consensus. However, common positions were not binding on the member states, although national governments did agree to avoid actions that might undermine common positions. The result of all this was some degree of streamlining of European foreign policies, albeit outside the realm of the community.

Not until the negotiations for the Maastricht Treaty in 1991 did a more coherent approach to European foreign policy emerge. The Treaty, as a result of the negotiations, introduced the three-pillar structure to the newly termed European Union,[3] which meant that the Common Foreign and Security Policy (CFSP) was now regarded as an official EU policy. Maastricht also added "joint actions" as another diplomatic weapon to the arsenal of the CFSP. Once adopted by consensus, common positions and joint actions were binding to the member states. Regarding defense, the Treaty mentioned the "eventual framing of a common defense policy, which might in time lead to a common defense," for the purpose of building up the WEU as the defense component of the EU, but also citing the WEU's future development as a way to strengthen the European pillar within NATO.

The Amsterdam Treaty further fleshed out the gradually developing defense plan by stating that the EU was now willing to launch the Petersberg tasks, to be implemented by the WEU.[4] The CFSP also introduced the post of High Representative—a position currently held by the former NATO secretary general Javier Solana. Another political step forward was to set up "common strategies" to give

Table 15.2. Common Foreign and Security Policy: Objectives and Instruments

Objectives

- Strengthen common values and interests, and the independence of EU security
- Preserve peace and strengthen international security
- Promote international cooperation
- Develop and consolidate democracy as well as the rule of law, human rights, and fundamental freedoms

Decisions Needed to Achieve Objectives

1. *Common Positions*: adopted by consensus and binding to all member states
2. *Common Strategies*: adopted by consensus and binding to all member states
3. *Joint Actions*: adopted under qualified majority voting in the Council of Ministers after prior unanimous agreement in the European Council

---

clearer focus to EU negotiations on the international stage. The newly introduced "constructive abstention" also allowed member states to voice disapproval of a particular position, strategy, or action without jeopardizing its overall implementation. One has to keep in mind, though, that the European Commission, the European Court of Justice, and indeed the European Parliament are largely sidelined from the foreign policy and security agenda.[5] CFSP is strictly the business of the Council of Ministers and the European Council, which is a purely intergovernmental approach to handling these matters.

The Franco-British St. Malo Initiative of 1998 added further strength to the CFSP. With the violent breakup of Yugoslavia still on their minds, Prime Minister Tony Blair and President Jacques Chirac agreed that the EU must have the capacity for autonomous military action through a credible military force of member states operating within the EU framework. St. Malo thus brought about the establishment of a European Security and Defense Policy (ESDP) that would be used for military missions where the United States did not intend to get involved, and that would freely use national military assets previously committed exclusively to NATO. The Helsinki summit of December 1999 formalized these ideas; it set a deadline for mounting a Rapid Reaction Force of fifty thousand to sixty thousand troops by 2003 that would be responsible for crisis management, peacekeeping, peacemaking, conflict prevention, and humanitarian and rescue missions.[6] The EU also agreed to establish a nonmilitary response capacity that today can provide the civilian component of crisis management with up to five thousand police officers, one thousand of whom can be deployed within thirty days.

The Nice summit in December 2000 formalized the institutions of the ESDP, including a political and security committee, a military committee, and military staff. In December 2003 the member states adopted a European Security Strategy giving top priority for action to the fight against terrorism, the strategy for achieving peace in the Middle East, and Bosnia-Herzegovina.

Table 15.3. Responsibilities of the Rapid Reaction Force

1. Be able to deploy within sixty days
2. Carry out its mission for at least one year
3. Maintain a strength of fifty thousand to sixty thousand thousand troops
4. Carry out humanitarian and rescue missions, conflict prevention, peacekeeping, and peacemaking

One has to keep in mind, though, that the Rapid Reaction Force is not a European army, since it relies only on the deployment of national troops. Further, the EU must obtain the approval of all NATO members to gain access to NATO's planning capabilities and other resources. In any case, one has to question the military effectiveness of a force comprised only of fifty thousand or sixty thousand troops. The UK, in fact, has argued that the force needs to be expanded in light of developments in the aftermath of the bombing of the World Trade Center in 2001.

Despite the organizational and structural impediments, the ESDP has made its mark in international politics. In January 2003 an EU police mission of five hundred officers relieved the UN International Police Task Force in Bosnia-Herzegovina. In further action, in April of that year the NATO force in Macedonia was replaced first by an EU military force and then by a two hundred-strong EU police mission. In December 2004 an EU military force (EUFOR) of eight thousand troops replaced the NATO-led Security Force in Bosnia-Herzegovina (SFOR).[7] In 2006 the EU sent thirty-five hundred troops to the Democratic Republic of Congo to help maintain stability during the presidential and parliamentary elections. Following the Israeli-Hezbollah clash in Lebanon during July and August 2006, a number of member states, led by France and Italy, contributed seventy-five hundred troops to strengthen UNIFIL, the UN's Interims Force in Lebanon.

Another advance in foreign policy came with the development of the European Neighbourhood Policy (ENP) in 2004. The ENP offers financial assistance to countries beyond the frontier of the EU, provided they meet the strict conditions of government reform, economic reform, and other issues surrounding positive transformation. The sixteen countries that comprise the ENP are Algeria, Armenia, Azerbaijan, Belarus, Egypt, Georgia, Israel, Jordan, Lebanon, Libya, Moldova, Morocco, the Palestinian Authority, Syria, Tunisia, and Ukraine.[8] The ENP focuses on the objectives of democracy and human rights, the rule of law, good governance, the market economy, and sustainable economic development. In return for a commitment to these goals, ENP countries receive substantial financial support from the European Neighborhood and Partnership Instrument (ENPI), which, between 2007 and 2013, will dispense 12 billion Euros.[9] With the exception of Syria, Belarus, and Libya, the EU (more precisely the European Council and the Council of Ministers) had agreed on specific action plans with thirteen entities by the end of 2006.

Assessment

A number of different institutions and individuals represent the EU abroad, strongly suggesting that the Union does not speak with a single authoritative voice on the international stage. What the non-European world sees are at least three different actors within the EU, none with central authority. The Commission, for example, exerts international influence as the EU's negotiator at the World Trade Organization by conducting enlargement processes and managing economic relations with third countries; the Council Presidency merely informs the world of the EU's positions; and, lastly, the High Representative for CFSP, who ought to act as the spokesperson for the General Affairs Council within the Council of Ministers, is decisive only if all member states have decided on a specific course of action. The problem identified by U.S. Secretary of State Henry Kissinger in the 1970s remains the same: Who do I call when I need to speak with Europe?

People's expectations of the EU's foreign policy may be too ambitious. The simple fact is that the Union is not a global superpower, although it certainly possesses the economic muscle to be one. The CFSP complements but does not replace the foreign policies of its member states, and this became all the more evident in 2003, when the EU could not agree on a strategy toward Saddam Hussein's Iraq. Although the UK, Spain, Poland, Italy, and Portugal supported George Bush's war effort, the other member states were reluctant to send troops, and the European Council of March 2003 could agree only on the wish for a "speedy conclusion to the hostilities."

Nonetheless, the EU has had a significant impact on a number of important world events. Not to be underestimated were the trade sanctions against apartheid South Africa and Slobodan Milosevic's Yugoslavia. The commercial attractiveness of the EU's Single Market exerts a discipline on the economies of non-EU countries that do not want to jeopardize their access to prosperous European markets. In relations with its eastern neighbors, including Russia, Ukraine, Moldova, and other countries in the south Caucasus and central Asia, the EU signed agreements covering trade, political cooperation, environmental protection, and scientific and cultural collaboration. With neighboring countries on the southern and eastern shores of the Mediterranean, the EU seeks to establish a free trade area as part of the so-called Barcelona Process.[10] The EU also remains a highly active player in Afghanistan and the occupied territories of Palestine. In Afghanistan, it both makes up the majority of the NATO-led international stabilization force in Kabul, and in 2002–2003 it offered a reconstruction package of 680 million Euros. For Palestine, the Union committed about 1 billion Euros in loans and grants between 1993 and 2001. Finally, the Union's progressive enlargement has played a role in persuading the candidate countries of Central and Eastern Europe to adhere to the Copenhagen criteria, especially the promotion of democracy and human rights.

In all the projects noted here, the EU has played a role in international politics, although often through quiet, yet persistent, processes. The ultimate test of this assessment will come in the shape of Turkey's envisaged integration into the Union. No foreign policy nor diplomatic effort could prompt such sweeping economic, social, political, and cultural transformations than those accession criteria that Brussels expects its easternmost candidate to fulfill.

Future Challenges Facing the CFSP

European states are no longer global powers. Today, at best, only Britain and France would risk an engagement abroad, whereas most other states, notably Germany, the economic power house of the EU, prefers a low-key approach to global affairs. However, the crises in Kosovo and in Macedonia showed that political and military activism by European states, particularly the UK, cannot necessarily be ruled out. It seems that an involvement by any EU member state or by the EU as a whole depends on where one draws the borders of Europe and the EU's sphere of influence. In the context of today's global security, the prospect of grand-scale external threats, like those experienced during the Cold War era, is likely a scenario of the past. Nowadays security threats emanate from ethnic animosities, aggressive nationalism, or terrorism. Hence there is a profound need for peacemaking and peacekeeping facilities that overrides the former notions of traditional warfare. Specially trained police and paramilitary forces will gain greater importance over traditional armies and weaponry. For the EU, this requires a clearer definition of "regional interests" and a more precisely defined agenda of CFSP goals. Specifically, an urgent need has emerged for a clear delineation of powers and responsibilities for NATO versus the EU, as well as a potential European army. Otherwise the ongoing arguments and negotiation over responsibilities and strategies will prevail: systematic confusion will continue over peacekeeping versus peacemaking, concerted action versus unilateral action, and whether NATO or a European army ought to take responsibility.

The breakup of Yugoslavia showed that the EU had failed to act promptly and responsibly because it lacked political cohesion, as well as efficient institutions and cogent instruments. The United States had had to step in, most notably in Bosnia-Herzegovina, and finally achieve stability through the Dayton agreements in 1995. Yugoslavia posed a severe test to the political rationale of the EU. Is it more than an economic union? Does it have a political and moral agenda? And, if so, how far is it willing to impose it? Is the EU ready to match its economic might by assuming global political responsibilities? The Union's tentative response in Yugoslavia, and NATO's bombing campaign against Serbia, brought these questions to the fore and caused mixed reactions and often disillusionment in the European public. The problem of Serbia clearly resulted in a loss of credibility for both NATO and the EU and its member state governments. On one hand, the Alliance dallied for a long time before finally intervening militarily, and, on the other, a swift and decisive intervention was undermined by the cumbersome decision-making process, such as the requirement to agree unanimously on bombing targets.

The EU intended to address these shortcomings through the establishment of the Rapid Reaction Force. It remains to be seen, however, whether the intergovernmental nature of this force and the requirement for unanimity might stand in the way of much needed proactivity of the EU in the international sphere. At the moment, it seems unlikely that the intergovernmental structure of the CFSP will ever result in a supranational European army. In fact, the CFSP could show us one of the end points of European integration, in which some form of cooperation between the member states is institutionalized, albeit without threatening national sovereignty.

16

Trade and the Common Commercial Policy

Shoes, pullovers, and food are just three areas in which trade policy has reached the headlines in recent years. The shoes and pullovers have concerned the effects of opening trade with China and the massive increase of cheap Chinese imports that are said to threaten the European shoe and textile industries. Food became an issue as a result of a trade dispute with the United States about whether genetically modified food can be allowed to enter European markets. Trade is not just an unimportant niche subject but goes to the heart of international relations, and especially relations between citizen and state when it involves public health concerns. Trade, of course, also affects relations between developed and developing countries: should European farmers receive subsidies and be protected by trade barriers that "block" imports from developing states? When the Treaty of Rome established the European Economic Community in 1957, all member states agreed to a common external tariff that largely ruled out national trade policies, such as quotas. With the establishment of the Single Market in 1986, the Common Commercial Policy (CCP) became crucial; without a CCP, non-EU exporters potentially could enter the EU market via the member state with the lowest tariff, and then exploit the free movement of goods to ship their products anywhere within the Union. Clearly the Single Market required a uniform approach to how European states trade with the rest of the world.

*The EU is the world's biggest trader[1] and at the same time has become an advo-
cate of multilateral trade. Although different member states have different traditions
in their approach to international trade, the EU's basic orientation has always been
liberal, aiming to achieve a relatively harmonious development in world trade and the
progressive abolition of trade barriers. The fear that the common external tariff would
lead to high trade barriers has not been justified so far. The overall effect of establishing
the European Community as a customs union has broadly created trade rather than
diverting it; that is, it has reduced tariffs among member states to a larger extent than
deterring third country imports because of tariff barriers. Given this history of EU trade
policy, this chapter aims to address the following issues:*

1. What explains the development of EU trade policy?
2. What impact does the EU have on the international economic system?
3. Should the EU collaborate or compete economically with the U.S.?

The Global Trade Regime

The international trade regime was one of the key pillars of international economic
cooperation after the Second World War. A significant step toward global free trade
was the Uruguay Round (1986–1993), which resulted in the latest version of the General Agreement on Tariffs and Trade (GATT) that brought agriculture and textiles
under a multilateral regime. GATT also regulated services through the General
Agreement on Trade in Services (GATS), intellectual property rights through the
General Agreement on Intellectual Property Rights (TRIPS), and trade relations
through the Trade Related Investment Issues (TRIM), while also establishing a
system whereby signatory countries agreed to a binding settlement of disputes.
The Uruguay agreement yielded a single package that for the first time organized
bilateral trade relations between countries within a uniform set of regulations that
did not grant opt-outs. Russia, China, and Switzerland, however, chose not to sign
the agreement.

As part of the Uruguay Round, GATT was transformed into the World Trade
Organization in 1995. Located in Geneva, the WTO regulates trade in goods, services, and intellectual property rights based on negotiations between the signatory
countries. Russia and Switzerland continued to stay outside the WTO, but China
joined in 2003. As in GATT, trade partners agree to the binding settlement of disputes, but in the WTO this includes official rulings by WTO law chambers.[2] Should
a dispute between trade partners arise—for instance, public health concerns over
food imports—the EU has to defend its position before the WTO and face potential
sanctions for noncompliance with its rulings.

The next round of trade negotiations took place in 2001, in Doha, the capital
of Qatar. Some states, particularly the U.S., aimed for further liberalization in agriculture and services. Developing countries, however, sought further liberalization

Table 16.1. Decision Making within the CCP

1. Setting objectives: Commission together with the Article 133 Committee
2. Negotiations: Trade Commissioner
3. Adoption of results: Council of Ministers

not only of agriculture but also of textiles, whereas the EU concentrated on environmental concerns, especially the recognition of the socio-cultural dimension of its agricultural sector. The subsequent summit in Cancun in 2003 exposed the difficulties in moving global trade further. The U.S. had just raised tariffs on steel, while also increasing agricultural subsidies. On the other hand, the EU struggled with the reform of its Common Agricultural Policy, and here, in particular, access of non-EU producers, and this resulted in a premature end to negotiations.[3]

Decision-Making Process

The overall decision-making process comprises three steps: set objectives, negotiate, and adopt the results.

1. *Setting objectives.* The Commission is required to present its trade objectives to, and have them endorsed by, the Article 133 Committee, which includes trade officials from the member states and usually meets with the Commission weekly. During these meetings, the full range of trade policy issues is discussed, and it is here that the Commission has to present its specific trade objectives and has to secure endorsement for these. In contrast to the U.S. Congress, the European Parliament is not actively involved in trade policy, and it debates trade issues only after the mandate has already been adopted by the Council of Ministers. The Commission, however, encourages interest groups to offer feedback and input during the development of the mandate.

2. *Negotiating.* The Commission, represented by its Trade Commissioner, is the negotiating authority at the WTO. Again, the Article 133 Committee is deeply involved in discussions and consultations during negotiations with third parties, thus reflecting the fundamental nature of the EU as a balance between intergovernmental and supranational forces.[4]

3. *Adopting results.* The results of negotiations must be approved by the Council of Ministers (in this case, the General Affairs and External Relations Council (GAERC), which brings together foreign ministers of member states). Adoption is through qualified majority voting (QMV) for trade in goods and through unanimity for trade in services or intellectual property rights. In practice, however, member states try to obtain consensus, particularly during the conclusion of WTO rounds or when sensitive national issues are at stake. The European Parliament has no power to adopt results but does have to approve association agreements with third countries.

Table 16.2. The Role of the European Commission (DG Trade)

- Define EU interests
- Negotiate agreements on behalf of EU member states
- Monitor implementation of international agreements
- Act as liaison with other departments within the Commission with a trade dimension (environment, competition, agriculture, etc.)
- Inform the public

The Nice Treaty entered into force in 2003, with a list of exclusions expressing some member states' reservations to expanding the Common Commercial Policy. Among the notable exclusions were that France could continue to protect its national film industry. Other exclusions concerned certain cultural and health care issues and matters of social policy and transport. Nice produced a compromise: the CCP integrated obligations that had been established in the Uruguay Round, including trade in services and intellectual property rights, but the nature of the exclusions indicate that the member states themselves, not the Commission, determine the contractual basis for international negotiations.

The Instruments of the CCP

The CCP uses various tools to implement the EU's trade agenda, for example, tariffs, quotas, voluntary export restraints (VER), anti-dumping measures, and trade sanctions.

1. *Tariffs.* The average EU tariff is about 4.2 percent for countries that have negotiated trade agreements with the EU. For agriculture, the tariff jumps to 16 percent and is even higher for specific products such as sugar, wheat, and dairy products. As much as 40 percent of imports, however, have no tariff. Tariff-free imports include construction materials, computers, and telecom equipment. Sensitive imports such as cars, clothing, or footwear have a 10 percent surcharge.

2. *Quotas.* The EU sets import limits on certain goods, primarily bananas, sardines, tuna, iron, and steel.

3. *Voluntary export restraints (VER).* Quantitative export restrictions are agreed upon jointly by exporters and importers. A well-known VER is the 2005 agreement limiting the quantity of Chinese textiles that can enter the EU.

4. *Anti-dumping measures.* Dumping refers to the practice of selling goods below the market price in order to gain a higher market share with the goal of harming competitors. The WTO allows for countervailing measures, such as the imposition of custom duties that are equivalent to the dumping margin. The Commission's responsibility is to check for evidence of dumping and decide the type of counteraction to take. An example of this is the Commission's response, in the 1980s, to the import of semiconductors and chemicals from the United States.

Table 16.3. Instruments of the CCP

1. Tariffs
2. Quotas
3. Voluntary export restraints
4. Anti-dumping Measures
5. Trade sanctions

5. *Trade sanctions.* The most obvious sanction is where the EU simply stops trading with a country altogether, mainly for political reasons. Notable examples are sanctions against South Africa in the 1980s and Milosevic's Yugoslavia in the 1990s. The Trade Barrier Regulation of 1994 gave WTO members the opportunity to act against unfair trade measures by, for example, preventing access to a particular market. A country can impose sanctions if it receives permission from the WTO. In the case of the EU, however, this is done with a QMV voting in the Council.

Trade Patterns

About 63 percent of the EU's overall trade is between EU member states. Some 45 percent of the EU's trade outside its own boundaries is with developed countries, and of these the most important are the United States, China, and Russia. Some 40 percent of trade is with lesser-developed countries. From a regional perspective, we recently witnessed the growing influence of Asia, and here in particular China with whom the EU has a negative trade balance of nearly 130 billion Euros (see Table 16.4). However, one has to keep in mind that 63 percent of the EU's overall trade actually happens between EU member states. Accusations that the EU has a nearly closed circle of trade partners are not necessarily unfounded.

Trade Agreements

The EU has no specific trade agreements with its major trading partners, including Japan and the United States. Trade with these partners is managed under the WTO rules. Beyond the WTO, the EU has negotiated trade relations with other partners in five trading areas: the European Economic Area (EEA); the Euro-Mediterranean Partnership; Association Agreements; agreements reached with the developing countries as part of the EU's Development Policy; and agreements with the wider world.

1. The *European Economic Area* is a bloc of states that accepts all directives and regulations emanating from the EU's Single Market program. In this respect, Norway, Iceland, and Liechtenstein implement EU law to gain access to the EU's Single Market.[5] Because these states are not EU countries, they cannot participate in the formulation of, for instance, product regulations. Instead, they simply follow EU regulations for ease of trade relations.

Table 16.4. The EU's Leading Trade Partners in 2006

EU imports from	Billion Euros	Percent	EU export partners	Billion Euros	Percent
World	1,364.0	100.0	World	1,189.1	100.0
1. China	192.5	14.1	1. U.S.	269.5	22.7
2. U.S.	179.2	13.1	2. Switzerland	87.9	7.4
3. Russia	137.2	10.1	3. Russia	71.9	6.0
4. Norway	79.1	5.8	4. China	63.9	5.4
5. Japan	76.6	5.6	5. Turkey	46.7	3.9

Source: Eurostat 2008.

2. The *Euro-Mediterranean Partnership* was launched in November 1995 at the Barcelona conference of EU foreign ministers and eleven non-EU counterparts from Mediterranean countries. The objective of the partnership, referred to as the Barcelona Declaration, is to form a free trade area by 2010 where there would be no tariff barriers such as technical specifications that prevent products from being exported to another country, and no agricultural barriers or obstacles to services. At first glance, this agreement looks promising for the region, as it potentially offers preferential access to rich European markets. On closer inspection, however, vital goods such as clothing and textiles are exempt. Furthermore, the industrial base of the Barcelona countries is rather small and does not pose a significant threat to EU producers.

3. *Association Agreements* allow a smooth integration of candidate countries into the EU. They are negotiated with each individual country and accommodate the acquis communautaire, as well as market access. As of 2008, the EU has three candidate countries: Croatia, Macedonia, and Turkey. The latter already signed a Customs Agreement as early as 1963, which was upgraded in 1996 to a Customs Union that nonetheless focused mainly on industrial goods and excluded the vital sectors of agriculture, services, and public procurement. The Association Agreement with Turkey is on a firmer footing, as negotiations for EU entry started in 2005. The importance of the EU for Turkey is unquestionable, with 58 percent of the country's exports going to Europe and 52 percent of its imports coming from an EU member state.

4. *Development Policy:* For nearly thirty years, trade relations with developing countries were dominated by the Lomē Conventions, named after the capital of Togo where the first Convention took place. Initiated in 1975, the agreement brought together the EU and forty-five states from Africa, the Pacific, and the Caribbean, the so-called ACP countries. Lomē aimed for an equal partnership and sought for a more just and balanced economic order. In the fields of agriculture, industrial development, and regional cooperation, the EU offered special aid for the least-developed countries. Even though by 2000 the ACP had expanded to seventy-one states, the Commission admitted that the Lomē Conventions had been a failure,

mainly because the policy was incapable of strengthening the industrial base of the developing world, and also failed to deliver on the promise of easier access to affluent European markets. Lomé was replaced in 2000 by the Cotonou Agreement (named after the capital of Benin), which, like its predecessor, concentrated on the seventy-eight ACP countries that had accumulated by 2005. Unlike its predecessor, the Cotonou Agreement provided for a transition to free trade through regional economic partnerships between developing countries. Access to Europe was still restricted for ACP countries, particularly in agriculture, although a new program that was launched in 2001 now grants the forty-nine poorest countries duty-free access to Europe. Cotonou was complemented by "Everything-But-Arms" agreements (EBA) that promised special aid and trade privileges to these countries once they met objectives of good governance and democracy. Thus an evident shift has occurred in how the EU relates to the developing world. At Lomé, the EU looked at development criteria such as GDP per capita and infant mortality rates; with Cotonou, the EU advocates general principles such as trade access, good governance, and economic diversity that can be achieved regardless of a country's economic development.

5. *The Wider World.* The EU has also reached trade agreements with Russia, the countries of the former Soviet Union, and South Africa, with the latter hoping to establish free trade. Starting in 2005 the EU was also negotiating a free-trade deal with the Gulf Cooperation Council (GCC), which includes Bahrain, Qatar, Saudi Arabia, Oman, Kuwait, and the United Arab Emirates. In Latin America, trade and cooperation agreements have been signed with Mexico and Chile, and the EU is also seeking trade liberalization with the Mercosur group, which includes Brazil, Argentina, Paraguay, and Uruguay. In December 2005 the EU granted duty- and quota-free access to an additional fifteen developing countries including Bolivia, Columbia, Peru, Ecuador, Venezuela, Costa Rica, Panama, Guatemala, El Salvador, Honduras, Nicaragua, Moldova, Georgia, Mongolia, and Sri Lanka.

Conclusion

Looking back on more than fifty years of European integration, the EU has clearly transformed the political and economic landscape of Europe. These five decades have witnessed some remarkable successes such as the creation of an internal market of 485 million consumers; some hitherto unimaginable projects, particularly the implementation of a single European currency; and also policies that have been widely criticized over the years, for example, the Common Agricultural Policy. Despite some setbacks, the European Union has delivered on its initial objectives of promoting economic prosperity and establishing peace on a war-ravaged continent.

In recent times, however, fundamental differences of opinion have appeared over the future of the EU. The failed 2005 referendums in the Netherlands and France on the ratification of the constitution, as well as the failed referendum in Ireland in 2008 on the Reform Treaty caused much consternation among the European political elites with voters, sending out the clear message that European integration either had gone far enough or had already gone too far. The issue of Turkey's future accession resulted in a further rift, as some member states are concerned about the political, economic, and institutional implications of integrating such a large country that is not only substantially below EU levels economically but also has distinctly different cultural and social standards.

We therefore ought to remind ourselves that Europe is not the European Union and that the European Union is not Europe. Instead, the EU is the organizational vehicle that aims to make sense of Europe with all its national differences and idiosyncrasies. For much of the second half of the twentieth century, European integration delivered through the EU made sense to the member states and the majority of their citizens, as national governments gave up some of their national sovereignty in order to achieve goals that could not be attained by the states individually. Once national governments no longer see the rationale of working with the EU for the sake of enhancing one's own national interests than the reason for the EU to exist in its current form will become questionable. Given the current doubts over the future course of European integration, one might want to examine other potential avenues. There are four possible options for the future shape of the EU.

United States of Europe. Altiero Spinelli and Jean Monnet's dream of a federal Europe along the lines of the United States has receded as the EU has enlarged. Their idea would call for a division of responsibilities between a central authority and states, regions, or provinces. This would mean closer integration in such fields as taxation, economic, foreign, and social policy. The original six founding states have traditionally advocated this model, although support for it has faded and only remains to some extent among the political elite in Luxembourg and Belgium. It is difficult to imagine a United States of Europe with an EU of twenty-seven or more member states.

Multi-Speed Europe. First introduced in the 1990s by the Germany politician Wolfgang Schäuble, and the former French foreign minister Dominique Strauss Kahn, this proposal would allow an inner core of countries (France, Germany, Belgium, the Netherlands, and Luxembourg) to move ahead with closer integration. This asymmetry among European partners already exists, given the single currency system, which does not include the UK, Sweden, and Denmark, and the Schengen agreement, which is not implemented by Ireland, Denmark, and the UK. In the future, it certainly remains possible that some member states will feel disappointed by the slow progress of the European project and decide to pursue their own common objectives for economic models that are more socially oriented than those promised by EU integration. We would then witness the start of a union within a union, thus introducing another organizational tier to the political landscape of the continent.

Free-Trade Europe. This concept has sometimes been called the British model of European integration. It argues that future European cooperation should be kept at an intergovernmental level, preferably with national vetoes. The cornerstone of this model is the Single Market, allowing for the free movement of goods and the removal of trade barriers. But any political form of integration, such as a more coherent foreign policy, is only possible with the unanimous consensus of member states. With the 2004 and 2007 enlargements and the pending integration of Turkey, Britain has won support for this idea, especially among countries such as Poland and Estonia that have more Atlanticist instincts and, at least in recent years, have placed greater emphasis on free markets than on social protection.

Constitutional Europe. Most recently advocated by the governments of Greece, Italy, and Spain, this proposal builds on the belief that the current EU is a formidable foundation but that it needs a European constitution that would allow significant institutional changes and also address some of the current lack of democratic features. In this view, the treaties of Maastricht, Amsterdam, and Nice, and maybe eventually the Reform Treaty, are regarded merely as individual bricks in the evolving process of building the European house.

Whatever the outcome of the current reform efforts, Europe needs an organizational framework, whether it is the EU or some other subsequent derivative. The European scene in the twenty-first century is vastly different from the divided world of the emerging Cold War of the 1950s, and the needs of European citizens and their governments have certainly changed. Global warming, technological innovation, the Internet, e-commerce, and other aspects of globalization have increased interdependencies between nations and are widely regarded as calling for close cooperation between states seeking to achieve common goals. Yet a closer and more integrated Europe will have to ensure that it does not undermine national differences and identities in the process. It remains to be seen whether the EU will be able to successfully perform this balancing act in the future.

Notes

1. Parameters of European Integration

1. It is important to note that the Council of Europe is not an EU institution. Similarly, the European Court of Human Rights in Strasbourg, which is related to the Council of Europe, should not be confused with the EU's European Court of Justice, which is located in Luxembourg.

2. Jean Monnet, a rather illustrious character, was born in France in 1888 and spent his early years working in his father's cognac business. He was not drafted in World War I because he suffered from nephritis. During World War II and after the fall of France in 1940, he worked for the UK government and was instrumental in organizing supplies for the French Resistance movement. Monnet died in March 1979 at the age of ninety.

3. The WEU began life as the Brussels Treaty Organization. The Brussels Treaty was signed on 17 March 1948 by Belgium, France, Luxembourg, the Netherlands, and the United Kingdom, and provided for collective self-defense and economic, social, and cultural collaboration between its signatories. In 1954 the Brussels Treaty was modified to include West Germany and Italy, thus creating the Western European Union. The WEU was primarily concerned with increasing Soviet control of Central and Eastern Europe, and committed all signatory countries to the mutual defense of any member.

4. The initial purpose of EURATOM was twofold: it sought to ensure the creation of the necessary conditions for the development of nuclear energy within the community and also worked to guarantee an equitable supply of ores and nuclear fuels. The treaty created the EURATOM Supply Agency, which had the power to purchase fuels for community use and develop a common supply policy based on the principle of equal access to fuel.

5. The Treaty of Rome also established the institutions of the EEC: an Assembly (renamed Parliament at its first meeting), the Council of Ministers, the Commission, and the Court of Justice. The balance between these institutions would evolve as the EEC developed, but the Treaty set an important precedent in securing a supranational decision-making institution in the Commission, while limiting the role of the Parliament and therefore the involvement of European citizens whom that institution ought to represent.

6. British interest in European integration was largely a product of the country's declining international political prominence, especially in the aftermath of the Suez crisis in 1956. By the end of the 1950s,

Britain also had to confront the fact that economic ties were shifting away from the Commonwealth toward the European continent.

7. The European Commission, the EU's key bureaucracy, is analyzed in detail in chapter 3.

8. Charles de Gaulle had been forced to leave office in 1969 at the age of seventy-nine, and his counterpart in West Germany, Chancellor Konrad Adenauer, resigned in 1963 at the age of eighty-seven.

9. According to the country's statistical office, West Germany's exports nearly trebled between 1960 and 1970, rising from 24.5 billion Euros (at 2004 prices) to 64 billion.

10. Luxembourg's prime minister, Pierre Werner, was commissioned to write a report on the suitability of an economic and monetary union. The report had a marked impact on the process of establishing the Euro in the 1990s. Chapter 13 offers a more detailed analysis of the Euro.

11. The Merger Treaty, which was signed in April 1965 and implemented on 1 July 1967, integrated the EEC, the ECSC, and EURATOM as the European Community.

12. This system was called "the snake," as the value of a national currency was allowed to fluctuate by 2.25 percent in either direction in relation to other national currencies. It was this continual fluctuation that inspired commentators to use the metaphor of a snake wiggling its way from one end of the scale to another; more on this in chapter 13.

13. With the election of Ronald Reagan in 1980, the U.S. underwent a drastic transformation of its macro-economic approach. The neo-liberal agenda of "Reaganomics" advocated tax cuts for big business and high-income earners, based on the premise that the subsequent savings would help boost productivity and employment levels. Through a "trickle-down effect," Reagan contended, the generated wealth would eventually reach broader segments of society. Reagan also argued for a limited role of the state in addressing and managing economic problems. Reagonomics was based on the monetarist philosophy of Milton Friedman, of the University of Chicago, who called for the state to be a passive actor, merely responsible for organizing and safeguarding the parameters within which economic activity and the free flow of market forces ought to take place. Reaganomics, therefore, was in stark contrast to prevailing European approaches that still relied to a significant extent on Keynesianism and its reliance on a much more interventionist and proactive role of the state.

14. The so-called cooperation procedure is explained in more detail in chapter 7.

15. More information about the so-called assent procedure is provided in chapter 7.

16. The full text of Thatcher's speech can be viewed on www.margaretthatcher.org/speeches.

17. The "co-decision procedure" was introduced by the TEU. In such policy fields as health, consumer protection, or culture, for instance, the EP now had veto power enabling it to block legislation. See also chapter 7.

18. The WEU never merged with the EU largely because the latter integrated member states that did not belong to NATO and considered themselves neutral. With the Amsterdam Treaty of 1997, the EU adopted the WEU's so-called Petersberg Tasks of peacemaking, peacekeeping, and humanitarian missions as the basis of a European security and defense policy. With the gradual development of the CFSP, the rationale of the WEU has been seriously questioned, and no significant activities, or indeed meetings, have taken place since 2001. See chapter 15.

19. With the Labour Party winning the elections in 1997, one of the first acts of Prime Minister Tony Blair was to join the social charter.

20. At a summit meeting in the Luxembourg town of Schengen, Belgium, the Netherlands, France, Luxembourg, and West Germany decided to remove all border controls between the signatory countries. The agreement came into force in 1985, and over the next years Spain, Portugal, and Italy joined up. Denmark, Ireland, and the UK, however, chose not to ratify the Schengen Agreement. In the case of the latter two, this decision was mainly prompted by fears over terrorism in Northern Ireland. By 2008 all EU member states with the exception of Britain, Ireland, Bulgaria, and Romania have ratified Schengen. Three non-EU states are also enrolled in the program: Iceland, Norway, and Switzerland.

21. EU citizenship is granted to those who have obtained citizenship status in one of the member states.

22. In June 2004 ten new members joined the Union: Cyprus, the Czech Republic, Estonia, Hungary, Latvia, Lithuania, Malta, Poland, Slovakia, and Slovenia. Romania and Bulgaria followed suit in 2007.

23. The so-called IGC consists of representatives of the governments of EU member states who meet at length to prepare the agenda for summit meetings. This system was first used during the negotiations over the Single European Act. The IGC for the summit meeting in Nice began on 7 February 2000 and ended with the agreement on the Treaty of Nice (7–11 December 2000).

24. The specific institutional changes are addressed in the individual chapters on the Commission (chapter 3), the Council of Ministers (chapter 5) and the European Parliament (chapter 7).

25. The Convention of Europe consisted of 105 representatives from all 15 member states, as well as from the 10 countries that were about to join in 2004.

2. Enlargement

1. The initial membership of EFTA in 1960 included Britain, Denmark, Portugal, Austria, Sweden, Norway, Switzerland, Finland, and Iceland. The microstate of Liechtenstein joined later on.

2. After the ousting, in Portugal, of the Caetano regime in 1974 and the death of Spain's General Franco in 1975, both countries applied for EU membership in 1977.

3. With the accession of Sweden, Austria, and Finland, and disregarding the microstates of Liechtenstein, Monaco, the Vatican, Andorra, and San Marino, only three West European countries remained outside the EU: Iceland, Norway, and Switzerland. Iceland considered membership at the time of the British accession in 1973 but concluded that policy differences, regarding fishing, in particular, were simply too great. Norway applied for membership in 1972 and 1992. Each time, however, a negative referendum voted to stay outside the EU, mainly because Norwegians thought that their country was already quite prosperous and well served by the existing free trade agreement with Brussels. Like Norway, the Swiss government also applied to the EU in 1992 but had to withdraw its application after a negative referendum. Thus EFTA continues to exist, with Iceland, Norway, Switzerland, and Liechtenstein as its members.

4. For more information, see chapter 11.

5. The programs designed to assist applicant countries in their development prior to joining the EU include the following:

- ISPA (Instrument for Structural Policies for Pre-Accession); invested around 1 billion Euros annually in transportation and the environment
- SAPARD (Special Program of Pre-Accession for Agriculture and Rural Development); invested around 500 million Euros annually
- Phare (Poland/Hungary Assistance for Reconstruction of Economies); invested around 1.5 billion Euros annually
- TAIEX (Technical Assistance Information Exchange Instrument); provideed information exchange on all aspects of the acquis communautaire
- Twinning; provided full-time secondment of advisers from the EU-15

6. These programs are discussed in greater detail in chapter 11.

7. For a more extensive discussion, see Christopher Preston, *Enlargement and Integration in the European Union* (London: Routledge, 1997).

8. The chief disagreement over British membership was the country's contribution to the EU budget. Successive prime ministers, particularly Margaret Thatcher, argued that Britain paid too much into Brussels' coffers, based mainly on the fact that the UK had a limited agricultural sector, the sector on which the EU spends most of his money. The issue was finally resolved at a summit meeting in Fontainebleau in 1984, which granted Britain a rebate of 60 percent of the difference between the money it paid into the budget (as a share of its GDP) and the money it received from redistributional programs. By 2005 this rebate came to more than 4 billion Euros. In light of the accession of much poorer states, the rebate became the subject of much controversy, with Central and Eastern European countries, Sweden, and the Netherlands, in particular, calling for an end to this preferential treatment. During the summit meeting of December 2005, Prime Minister Tony Blair eventually gave in to mounting diplomatic pressure and agreed to reduce the rebate to 1 billion Euros.

9. One element of these principles is the EU's commitment to the prohibition of the death penalty.

10. Ethnic tensions between Greek and Turkish Cypriots reached a violent climax in 1974 which forced the Turkish army to intervene. The invasion resulted in the de-facto division of the island, with Greek Cypriots in the southern part and Turkish Cypriots in the northern part, where the Turkish army continues to have a sizable military presence. Aside from Turkey, no other country has ever given diplomatic recognition to the self-styled Turkish Republic of Northern Cyprus (TRNC).

11. The province of Kosovo was under Serbian control until 1999, when a NATO-led intervention came to the rescue of a predominantly ethnic Albanian population. Since that time, Kosovo is under the administration of the UN Mission in Kosovo (UNMIK). In 2007, the UN envoy Marti Ahtisaari proposed full independence for the province with protective rights for the minority of ethnic Serbs. The Serbian government (as well as the majority of Serbian public opinion) rejected the proposal. The government of Kosovo declared independence in February 2008. Within the EU, France, the UK, and Germany are backing independence, while Greece, Romania and Cyprus are not. At the time of this writing, Russia stated that it will use its veto in the Security Council to prevent Kosovo's admission into the United Nations.

12. In a referendum in May 2006, Montenegro formed an independent country and left the state union with Serbia. In the run up to the referendum, as well as after it, the government indicated that it regards the country as a future EU candidate state. It therefore came as no surprise that negotiations on a Stabilization and Association Agreement began shortly thereafter.

13. The aims of the Stabilization and Association Process are the following:

1. The drafting of SAAs, with a view to accession
2. The development of economic and trade relations with the region and withinthe region
3. The development of the existing economic and financial aid
4. Aid for democratization, civil society, education, and institutional development
5. Cooperation in the field of justice and home affairs;
6. The development of political dialogue.

14. Commission Briefing, 18 January 2006.

3. The European Commission

1. Before the accession of Central and Eastern European states in 2004, the Commission was comprised of twenty individuals; nineteen commissioners and one Commission president. In a union of fifteen members, the five biggest states—France, Germany, the UK, Spain, and Italy—each had two commissioners, and all the others had one. The Treaty of Nice, which was designed to prepare the Union for enlargement, developed a new formula whereby each member state now only has one commissioner. The treaty also stated, however, that there could be no more than twenty-seven commissioners. Thus, should the union integrate additional members, some states might have to share a commissioner, but the treaty did not specify how such a rotating system might work. The most recent "reform treaty," rejected by the Irish public in June 2008, would have reduced the number of commissioners even further: to 15 from 2014 onwards.

2. The European Parliament also must approve the entire Commission. See chapter 7.

3. The appointment of Germany's commissioner Guenther Verheugen to the Enterprise and Industry portfolio in 2004 illustrates this point.

4. A telling example was the appointment of the Hungarian candidate Laszlo Kovacs in 2004. The member states decided that Hungary should be given the Energy portfolio, and the Hungarian government appointed Kovacs to this post. During his confirmation hearing before the European Parliament, however, it emerged that Kovacs had a rather thin knowledge of energy matters, and he was subsequently transferred to the portfolio of Taxation and Customs.

5. Walter Hallstein from West Germany, the first Commission president (1958–1967) and Jacques Delors from France (1985–1994) arguably have been the most influential individuals chairing this institution.

Both had a clear vision. Hallstein argued for a more federal Europe for which he was passionately opposed by French president Charles de Gaulle. Delors envisioned a "social Europe" that, in addition to the Single Market, also offered protection for workers; more than once, this vision resulted in acrimonious confrontations between Delors and Margaret Thatcher.

6. In addition to the Commission's services, there are eighteen European Community agencies, for example, the European Food Agency Authority, the European Railway Agency, and the European Environment Agency. Furthermore, there are three CFSP agencies, including the European Defense Agency, the EU Institute for Security Studies, and the EU Satellite Center. The responsibilities of all these services are to accomplish specific technical, scientific, or managerial tasks. Regarding JHA, two other agencies work to enhance cooperation between, customs, police, immigration, and justice departments in all member states.

7. The Prodi Commission (1999–2004) embarked on an ambitious program to reform the organization. Its key objective was the implementation of a new career development structure in which promotion is exclusively based on merit and performance. The new staff regulations took effect under the Barroso Commission in November 2004, and only the future will tell whether the innovations are effective.

8. Over the years the Commission has met with severe criticism because of its authority to issue rules of every nature, for example, deciding on the precise shape and size of cucumbers or the length of a sausage. The institution is perceived by many as overly bureaucratic, and this has resulted in growing public hostility.

9. Budget contributions could be raised to 1.27 percent of the GNP, but member states have decided that currently 1.045 percent is sufficient.

10. It is important to note that although the member states first give the Commission the negotiating parameters, the final agreement at WTO negotiations must still be endorsed by the member states based on the system of qualified majority voting (see chapter 5).

4. The European Council

1. Until 2003 the EU always met in the country holding the Presidency, which explains why EU treaties often had the name of a town attached to them, such as Amsterdam or Maastricht, as it was in those locations where the Summit took place. Since then, security considerations forced the member states to conduct at least some of their gatherings in Brussels.

2. A telling example of the opportunities given to a country that holds the Presidency was the Summit in Lisbon in March 2000. Later termed the "Dot.com Summit," the EU agreed on a complex set of measures with the aim of becoming the world's most competitive, knowledge-based economy by 2010.

3. Some meetings of the European Council stand out as definitive turning points in the history of the Union, for example, Bremen 1978, with the launching of the European Monetary System; Fontainebleau 1984, where the British budget rebate was resolved; and Maastricht 1991, Amsterdam 1997, and Nice 2000, where agreements were reached on the respective treaties.

4. The meeting in Nice in December 2000, however, surpassed all previous summits in length and political controversy. Instead of the usual two days, member states bargained for four days, especially, in view of enlargement, over the future of policies involving cohesion, the budget, and agriculture. The reweighing of national votes and the configuration of majority voting in the Council of Ministers was another important item on the agenda.

5. With a union of twenty-seven members, all with diverging opinions over the precise course for European integration, a unanimous communiqué might be impossible to reach. Therefore, some member states now commonly issue explicitly stated reservations.

5. The Council of Ministers

1. The Council of Ministers is officially called the Council of the European Union, an unfortunate choice as the name is similar to the Council of Europe, an international organization, not part of the

EU, that deals with human rights, and to the European Council, the summit where twenty-seven heads of government gather.

2. Coreper is an acronym for the French name of the committee, *Committee des Representatives Permanentes*.

3. The most recent reform of this complicated procedure was decided at the Nice Summit in December 2000. In lengthy bargaining processes, the member states tried to establish a formula which would allocate votes for every new member state that joined the EU in 2004, as well as for Romania and Bulgaria, which joined in 2007. With twenty-seven countries casting their votes, a fine balance had to be established safeguarding the interests of smaller member states while also guaranteeing significant progress toward greater European integration. Particular attention was paid to ensure that a country's population was reflected in the number of votes allotted. As the most populous country in the EU, Germany, home to some 80 million citizens, argued for a higher number of votes in comparison with France, with a population of only some 60 million. However, President Chirac argued that France should have identical voting powers in order to symbolize the equality between the two traditional driving forces of Europe. Poland, which had been invited to attend the Summit though not yet a member state, felt short-changed when a proposal was circulated that gave the country fewer votes than Spain, although both have nearly identical populations of some 40 million. In the end, after many late-night bargaining sessions, a resolution was reached. The Polish delegation was appeased by being granted the same number of votes as Spain, and German Chancellor Schröder backed away from his initial demand for the sake of European cooperation.

4. The Council of Ministers also has exclusive executive authorities over issues relating to the Euro and EMU (see chapter 13), where the Ecofin Council is effectively the economic government of the EU. Other councils, however, such as the Agriculture or Environment Council, have generally delegated all executive power to the Commission and merely fulfill their legislative duties by voting on proposals that emanate from the Commission.

6. The Presidency

1. The concept of a "troika" was introduced in 1981, whereby the foreign ministers of the current Presidency, of the one immediately preceding it, and of the immediate successor would meet to discuss political matters. Initially these meetings were merely briefings and lacked political substance, but since the Treaty of Amsterdam, in 1997, a great deal of coordination has been seen between successive presidencies.

2. The constitution also stated that the president would be appointed by the member states for a period of two and a half years, and would reside in Brussels.

7. The European Parliament

1. The Committee on the Environment, Public Health, and Food Safety, as well as the Committee on Budgetary Control are the most influential, since the EP exercises considerable power in these policy areas. On the other hand, the Committee on Transport and Tourism has always been marginal.

2. Legislation under a single majority is passed, when the majority of parliamentarians present are voting in favor of a proposal. However, the EP applies a system of absolute majority, where the majority of all MEPs (whether present or absent) must vote in favor for the legislation to pass. With the current membership at 785 MEPs, the absolute majority is 393.

3. For a record of attendance at voting sessions, see www.europarliament.net. In 2000 the turnout was 75 percent, whereas between 2001 and 2003 figures reached an average of 84 percent.

4. In contrast to co-decision, the assent procedure does not give the EP the right to make amendments; it either has to accept or reject the measure.

5. In the late 1980s the EP twice used the assent procedure to promote human rights by blocking protocols to the Turkish and Israeli association agreements. In 1992 the EP blocked 468 million ECU worth of aid to Morocco and 140 million ECU to Syria on human rights grounds.

6. Other commentators, such as Moravcsik and Majore, contend that the notion of a democratic deficit in the EU is a myth, arguing that, because the EU is not a state, it should not be subject to the same democratic demands as traditional states are. Moreover, both authors point to the fact that the EU specializes in areas in which direct democratic accountability is generally limited (for example, EMU and the role of the European Central Bank).

8. The European Court of Justice

1. The ECJ, however, is excluded from the vast majority of rulings in Pillar II of the Maastricht Treaty (Common Foreign and Security Policy) and most of Pillar III (Justice and Home affairs).

2. For example, the ECJ caseload jumped from 79 in 1970 to 433 in 1985, and the average length of proceedings for a ruling rose from six months in 1975 to fourteen months in 1985. As a result, the backlog of cases increased from 100 in 1970 to 527 in 1985.

3. For a more detailed analysis of the impact of EC case law, please see D. Dinan, *Ever Closer Union: An Introduction to European Integration* (New York: Palgrave Macmillan, 2005), chap. 10.

4. Fundamental rights can be categorized roughly into three groups: civil rights, such as respect for private life, freedom of religion, and freedom of expression; economic rights, such as the right to own property or the right to carry out economic activities; and rights of defense, such as the right to effective judicial remedy or the right to legal assistance.

5. Yvonne van Duyn was a Dutch national who had come to the UK to accept an offer of employment with the Church of Scientology. Van Duyn was refused entry to the UK on the grounds that the British government regarded the Church as socially harmful, although no legal restrictions were placed on its practices. Mrs. van Duyn took the UK Home Office to court, but, unfortunately for her, there was an EC directive giving the member state a degree of discretion, if the activity in question was contrary to public order. In effect, Mrs. van Duyn was not permitted to work in the UK on the grounds that the British government considered the Church of Scientology to be harmful and antisocial, and thus against the public order. With this ruling, however, the ECJ was able to advance its case law with numerous references to the free movement of people. In fact, this case enabled the Court to establish a precedent by upholding an individual's right to take up employment in another member state under the same conditions as a national of that state.

6. The German supermarket chain Rewe intended to import the French liqueur Cassis into Germany. But the German authorities refused to allow it, because the drink was not of sufficient alcoholic strength to be marketed as a liqueur. Under German law, liqueur had to have an alcoholic content of 25 percent, whereas Cassis only had between 15 and 20 percent. Rewe argued that the rule was a quantitative restriction, which runs counter to Article 30. The ECJ ruled that once a product has been lawfully produced and marketed in one member state it should be admitted into any other state without restrictions.

7. Gabrielle Defrenne—an airhostess with the Belgian airline Sabena—brought an action for compensation on the ground of discrimination of pay. Sabena did not dispute that male employees earned more money for the same type of work. The question referred to the ECJ was whether Article 119 (equal pay for equal work) had a direct effect on the airline. Of course, Van Gend en Loos already showed us that it had. The ECJ stated that the aim of Article 119 was the elimination of all discrimination, not only regarding individual undertakings but also entire branches of industries and even of the economic system as a whole. Subsequently, the Court's rulings on equal pay enabled the Commission to implement a series of directives on women's issues that forced the member states to end blatant discrimination in the workplace. This case was then followed by a series of cases dealing with pensions, training, part-time work, and so forth.

9. Checks and Balances

1. The Italian candidate Rocco Buttiglione was heavily criticized for remarks about homosexuality and single mothers, and Ingrid Udre from Latvia was charged with corruption and deemed unfit. Further, the Hungarian Lazlo Kovacs was judged by the EP as lacking the expertise needed to handle the

Energy portfolio. As a result of these censures, the EP threatened to disapprove of the entire Commission. Ultimately the Barroso Commission relented to the pressure: Buttiglione was replaced by Italy's former Europe Minister Franco Frattini; Kovacs was moved from Energy to Taxation; and Udre was replaced by her compatriot, Andris Piebalgs, who assumed responsibility for the Energy portfolio.

2. A good example may be seen in the current British Commissioner for Trade Peter Mandelson, a close political ally of former prime minister Blair. Mandelson's position as a national politician became untenable after he was forced to resign twice as a government minister.

3. The failed constitution of 2005 proposed that television cameras be allowed at Council meetings.

4. See also chapter 5.

10. The Single Market and Competition

1. The Commission acknowledged that uniformity across the EU in sensitive issues such as drugs, terrorism, and tax regimes was not on the agenda.

2. Member states, in the end, agreed on a minimum rate (now 15 percent) but failed to establish a maximum ceiling. Currently Finland has the highest VAT rate at 22.5 percent.

3. In terms of realistic consumer behavior, however, substantial national differences remained. For example, a Dutch person is far more likely to purchase goods in a Dutch shop than in a German shop, even if he or she lives on the Dutch-German border within equal walking distance from a Dutch and a German supermarket.

4. Prompted by the deregulation and privatization of key industries, the Commission estimated the following price reductions:

> Airfares: 41 percent between 1992 and 2000
> Electricity prices: 15 percent
> National telephone calls: 50 percent since 1998
> International telephone calls: 40 percent since 1998

5. In 2002, the EU had a population of 360 million people. This meant that geographical mobility was still rather limited, since only 4.6 percent of EU citizens lived in member states other than their country of origin.

6. See A. El-Agraa. *The European Union: Economics and Policies* (Upper Saddle River, N.J.: Prentice Hall, 2004), 195.

7. One can follow the progress of the Single Market by checking out the DG Internal Market's Web site: europa.eu.int. Click on activities, then "Internal Market," and then "Single Market Scoreboard."

8. The open method of coordination is based on benchmarking and targets. Member states not only agree on EU wide targets but also report on the progress of their national programs in achieving those targets. This method also allowed for policy learning through comparison. What became widely know as "Lisbon," therefore, relied on voluntary compliance by member states to targets set among themselves. The role of the European Commission had been marginalized to that of an overall secretariat. Given this approach, "Lisbon" therefore hardly threatened an invasion into sensitive national policies through further European legislation.

9. The directive was originally drafted by the Dutch Commissioner Frits Boltkestein in 2004, who served under the Prodi Commission from 1999 to 2004.

10. A wide range of services are free from regulatory restrictions and can be offered anywhere in the EU, regardless of where the business is registered, for instance, tourism and leisure businesses or business services such as consultancy work. However, services of "general economic interest," such as post, water, electricity, and waste, must be registered in the country where the service is delivered. Furthermore, national authorities have the right to regulate audiovisual services, gambling, lotteries, the activities of public authorities such as notaries, for instance, health care, social services, and other "non-economic services of general interest." Finally, industries that already have EU legislation in place,

including telecommunications, transport, and financial services, are not at all affected by this directive. Although a decision on the service directive was reached in November 2006, it will not become effective until the beginning of 2010.

11. L. McGowan and S.Wilks, "The First Supranational Policy in the EU," *European Journal of Political Research* 28, no. 2 (1995): 141–169.

12. "Positive integration" refers here to the creation of new policies at the European level, whereas "negative integration" means the mere removal of national rules.

11. Regional Policy and Cohesion

1. The geographical area stretching from London, to Paris, to Milan, and then back via Munich and Brussels roughly resembles a banana, and hence the name "blue banana."

2. The Cohesion system, which consists of a multitude of funds with different objectives and program guidelines, was often criticized for its complexity prior to 2007. Therefore, for the budget period 2007–2013, the goal of the Commission was to make the system more coherent.

3. The eligibility for convergence projects is limited to regions with less than 75 percent of the EU's average GDP.

4. All regions are eligible for this spending category except those that qualify for the convergence category (i.e., below the 75 percent threshold).

5. Eligible regions include those that share internal borders, external borders, or sea borders.

6. EU cohesion policy also applies to the eighteen "statistical effect" regions that were below the 75 percent threshold prior to the 2004 enlargement, but following enlargement and the subsequent drop in the EU's average GDP no longer qualified. Without transitional funding, these regions would justifiably feel punished for agreeing to the accession of the twelve new members. Hence the European Council agreed to support these regions to the amount of some 22 billion Euros. Furthermore, spending targets were set in order to support the long-term creation of jobs in such areas as research and innovation, the information society, and sustainable development. In the case of the Convergence objective, the target is 60 percent, and in the case of the Regional Competitiveness and Employment objective, the target is 75 percent of the total available funding.

7. Countries eligible for money from the Cohesion Fund include the twelve new Member States that joined in 2004 and 2007, and also Greece and Portugal. Spain's eligibility is transitional and will gradually be phased out.

8. Agreements for cohesion are reached by unanimity voting in the Council of Ministers.

9. A notable exception to the working mechanisms of this triangle are the so-called Community Initiatives which dramatically enhance the Commission's power and responsibility. Here, the Commission, not the Council of Ministers, is responsible for the design of policy measures and the general allocation of money, giving it the sole agenda-setting power.

10. These programs included ISPA, which offered support for investment in transport and the environment; SAPARD, the Accession Program for Agriculture and Rural Development with the aim of improving processing structures, marketing channels, and food-quality control; and *Phare*, which, since 1989, has focused on institution building and support for investment.

11. For a debate on the positive versus the negative effects of EU Cohesion, see R. Leonardi, "Cohesion in the European Community," *West European Politics* 16, no. 4 (1993): 492–515; and M. Keating, "A Comment on Leonardi," *West European Politics* 18, no. 2 (1995): 408–412.

12. The Common Agricultural Policy

1. As a general rule, all decisions on prices are based on unanimous consensus, although de jure, the Council's decision on agricultural measures is by qualified majority voting.

2. For a detailed discussion on the shortcomings of the CAP, see D. Dinan, *Ever Closer Union: An Introduction to European Integration* (New York: Palgrave Macmillan, 2005), 359–360.

3. For example, in that period production grew by 2 percent per annum, whereas the EU consumer purchased only an additional 0.5 percent of agricultural products.

4. A telling example is the Duke of Westminster, who owns prime real estate in central London and also runs a 1,280-acre farm in northwest England. With an estimated fortune of 4.9 billion£ (around 6.4 billion Euros), the duke, in 2004, nonetheless received a subsidy of 326,000£ (around 425 million Euros) from the EU budget.

5. See also Neill Nugent, *The Government and Politics of the European Union* (New York: MacMillan, 2006), 471–473.

6. These socio-cultural considerations require further clarification. If support for agriculture were to cease, many farmers might be forced to sell their farms and ultimately move to towns and cities, leaving their land either idle or to be taken over by bigger farms. Europe would then witness the transformation of its countryside along American lines, with acre upon acre of identical crops farmed by big agro-businesses stretching toward the horizon. The diverse European landscape would become a distant memory. Further, agriculture is quite often one of the few employment opportunities in rural areas. Without local jobs available, people would either have to commute, considerably impacting the environment, or move altogether to more urban areas, seriously undermining the economic and social livelihood of smaller communities. Schools and shops would then have to close, and a village might turn into a dormitory for the retired or second-home owners. For all these reasons European leaders often justify the high costs and trade distorting nature of the CAP.

7. ECU refers to the European Currency Unit, a basket of European currencies used as a means of settlement between European central banks. See also chapter 13.

8. In 1994, for instance, agriculture contributed less than 1 percent to the overall GDP in Luxembourg, Germany, and the UK; the share in France was 2 percent; and Greece had the highest rate at 7.5 percent (source: Eurostat).

9. In 1992 the EU overproduced 20 million tons of cereal, 1 million ton of dairy produce, and 750,000 tons of beef.

10. For example, the intervention price for cereals dropped by 29 percent; for beef, 15 percent; and for butter, 5 percent.

11. Large farmers were asked to set aside 15 percent of their arable land.

12. MacSharry established a program that subsidized farmers for up to twenty years if they set aside land to protect the environment.

13. One hectare equals 100 square meters, or around 300 square feet.

14. Price supports were reduced by 20 percent from the 1986–88 figures and export subsidies were gradually reduced by 36 percent by 2000.

15. For instance, the price for cereals was reduced by 20 percent and that of beef by 30 percent.

16. Ultimately the Berlin summit could only agree on a milk price reduction of 15 percent, and only to become effective in 2005. Beef prices were reduced by 20 percent, instead of the proposed 30 percent, and the price of cereals was reduced by a mere 7.5 percent.

17. The EU argued for a worldwide cut in trade-distorting subsidies by 55 percent and for lowering export refunds by an average of 45 percent, with a reduction of import tariffs by an average of 36 percent.

18. Fischler also proposed that rural development measures be introduced, 80 percent of which would be financed by the EU, including early retirement, afforestation, technical assistance, and environmental programs. He also envisioned the retraining of farmers for other professions to be financed by the Structural Funds of the Cohesion Policy (see chapter 11). Finally, Fischler offered the governments of the accession countries the chance for national top-ups to match these countries' spending levels on agriculture prior to joining the EU.

19. For 2004, for example, 44.4 billion Euros was earmarked for agriculture, and 30.7 billion Euros for Cohesion.

20. Specifically, the Fischler plan argued for a further reduction in price support. Farmers would now receive a flat rate of direct support based on their previous income, which should be reduced by 20 percent between 2004 and 2009. Also, under cross compliance, farmers would receive direct support once they met environmental and food safety standards, with a maximum financial aid of 300,000 Euros.

21. Farmer unions across Europe have been highly critical of the cross compliance system. Although most agreed that the old price support system was outdated and needed drastic reform, the new system, they felt, imposed a heavy bureaucratic burden with its numerous, detailed rules, for example, specifying the type of taps allowed for milk tanks and that oil tanks had to be blue and diesel tanks green.

22. A group of experts appointed by Commission President Prodi (Sapir Report 2003) argued that the CAP should be wound down and re-nationalized.

23. For more on COPA, see www.cogeca.be.

13. Economic and Monetary Union

1. Two power-generation projects of the New Deal were the development of the Tennessee Valley Authority and the building of Nevada's Hoover Dam.

2. Keynesianism has often encountered the problem that, during economic downturns, people may be reluctant to spend, and therefore reinvest in the economy, preferring instead to save their earned money for a rainy day. Similarly, a positive investment climate also depends to a significant extent on trust and the belief that governments can manage the economy successfully. But not every government automatically has such support. On top of this, the management of such large-scale projects requires a massive administrative effort, with the potential pitfalls of mismanagement and excessive bureaucracy. Most important is that Keynesian economic policies might require time to come to full fruition. During that lag, the economy might pick up, and thus government intervention would only accelerate a boom and cause inflationary pressures.

3. U.S. president Ronald Reagan (1981–89) and British prime minister Margaret Thatcher (1979–90), among many, were true believers in monetarism. Both implemented a series of tax breaks while also reducing public spending, which in the case of the U.S., however, was more than compensated by massive investment in the military.

4. Private banks can borrow money from a central bank that charges interest at their official rate. Private banks then utilize this as capital to pass on to their customers, thereby making a profit as these consumer loans are charged at a higher rate than the central bank rate. Hence a low interest rate will boost the economy as it allows for cheaper consumer loans, but with the added danger of a rise in prices as more money enters the economy. Conversely, higher interest rates can be used to lessen the inflationary tendencies in a rising economy since consumer spending will be curtailed by higher loan rates.

5. Every private bank is required to deposit a specified amount of money as a reserve at a central bank without earning interest. A higher minimum reserve will have a cooling effect on the economy as less money is available for consumer loans. A lower reserve, in turn, will boost consumer spending.

6. Prior to German unification in 1990 the Deutschmark was already the leading currency in Europe, and countries such as Denmark, the Netherlands, Austria, and Sweden had pegged their currencies to Germany's. A monetary union that integrated Germany's economic might was therefore highly attractive to European countries with weaker currencies, particularly France and Italy.

7. Once the UK, Spain, and Italy decided to participate in the EMS, the margins for these three countries were raised plus or minus 6 percent.

8. Because of this currency basket, every participating national currency contributed to a constantly changing value of the ECU. Businesses and private individuals could open bank accounts and, for example, invoice their clients in ECU. With some currencies going up and others going down, the currency volatility of the ECU was much less prominent than that of only a single national currency. The EMS also established a European Monetary Fund, which offered loan facilities for balance of payment assistance that was backed by 20 percent of national gold and U.S. dollar reserves, as well as 20 percent of national currencies.

9. On that day, which has since been named Black Wednesday, the British pound lost some 13 percent in value compared to the Deutschmark. This happened despite the massive infusion of 30 billion U.S. dollars by the Bank of England to keep up the value of the pound. In the end Britain plunged into a recession, and Black Wednesday was estimated to have resulted in job losses approaching one million.

10. The ECB has an Executive Board, with a president, vice president, and four other leading experts, that is appointed by the European Council for eight years. The role of the Executive Board is to implement

monetary policy. The Governing Council of the ECB, comprised of the Executive Board and governors of national central banks, sets interest rates. In addition to this is the General Council, made up of the Governing Council and governors of other European central banks that are not in EMU, which addresses tasks involving all EU states such as standardized accounting.

11. A negative referendum in Denmark in 2001 underlined the government's decision not to participate. Likewise, in the UK, public opinion is predominately against the Euro, and this opinion is supported by Tony Blair's successor and the former chancellor Gordon Brown, who stated that the country's economic structure is not yet in line with that of the Eurozone.

12. The countries were Finland, Germany, the Netherlands, Belgium, Luxembourg, France, Spain, Portugal, Austria, Ireland, and Italy.

13. The case of the exchange rate between the British pound and the Deutschmark is a telling one. During the 1990s the value of the pound fluctuated between 2.20 and 3.50 Deutschmarks. Businesses trading in both countries, therefore, were forced to set aside capital to compensate for potential losses arising from negative developments in the exchange rate that, in some cases, could amount to 20 percent of a business's annual turnover. With EMU, this tied-up capital could now be used to better effect.

14. In Italy, for instance, 1,936 lira equated to 1 Euro. If the price for a cappuccino was now 60 cents instead of 1,200 lira, customers almost automatically perceived this as cheap. In this instance, then, a café owner might have been prompted to raise the price to 80 cents (or 1,548 lira). In Germany, the business association for the gastronomical trade defended the price increases, arguing that many of their members had not printed new menus in anticipation of the introduction of the Euro. The association further argued that they would like to spare a further price update, and hence a new printed version of the menu. Therefore, prices were raised even further to account for the post-introduction period.

15. An illustration is offered by the economic boom in Ireland. Ever since the 1980s, the country has been enjoying an unprecedented economic expansion accompanied by inflation. With inflation for property, for instance, reaching such high levels that large sections of society have been priced out of the housing market, what Ireland needs are higher interest rates to slow the expansion. On the other hand, for years after the introduction of the Euro, France and Germany were suffering from an economic slowdown and could have done with lower interest rates than the ECB had agreed to. All these countries now had to apply non-monetary means to reach their economic ends.

16. Portugal made drastic budget cuts in order to fulfill the Stability Pact criteria. But between 2002 and 2007 France and Germany have persistently breached the pact with spending levels regularly exceeding 3.5 percent. Although the Commission can recommend fining a country that violates the Stability Pact, it has refrained from doing so mainly because such action would undermine investors' confidence in Europe's currency.

17. Granted, the EU is trying to offset this negative impact of EMU by financing cohesion. However, the total amount available for cohesion (some 30 billion Euros per year) does not seem overly generous for a union of 485 million citizens. See also chapter 11.

14. Justice and Home Affairs

1. The Trevi Group was named after the location where the group first met, a hotel directly opposite the famous fountain in the old town center of Rome. Trevi subsequently became the French acronym for *terrorisme, radicalisme, extremisme, et violence internationale.*

2. Regarding police and judicial cooperation in criminal matters (Pillar III), the powers of the European Court of Justice and the European Parliament were still severely curtailed. The EP was only consulted on legislative proposals without having a proper veto or agenda-setting power, and the ECJ also did not have the same powers that it wielded under Pillar I. For instance, the ECJ had no jurisdiction to review the legality of police operations.

3. For a summary of more recent JHA development, see J. D. Occhipinti, "Police and Judicial Cooperation," in *Developments in the European Union 2,* ed. M. Green Cowles and D. Dinan (New York: Palgrave Macmillan, 2004), 181–199.

4. This means that an Italian national living in Vienna, Austria, could theoretically be elected as mayor. That individual could also vote in local elections in Vienna and for the Viennese representative to the European Parliament. The Italian, however, is not allowed to stand or vote for any Austrian federal or regional government unless he or she assumes Austrian citizenship.

5. For a list of foreign populations and asylum applications for each member state, see V. Guiraudon, "Immigration and Asylum: A High Politics Agenda," in Cowles and Dinan, *Developments in the European Union 2*, 163.

6. Every member state agreed to examine the application of any alien and to pass on an asylum application to the member state that played the most important part in the applicant's entry or residence. Meanwhile, the responsible member state would take charge of the applicant throughout this period and allow the return of an applicant who is illegally in another member state.

7. It is important to remember that asylum and immigration policies are not applicable in all EU member states. For instance, Denmark opted out of JHA treaty provisions, and the UK and Ireland decide on their involvement on a case-by-case basis.

8. FRONTEX is located in Warsaw, Poland, and offers a means for member states to cooperate in managing external borders. The agency assists member states in training national border guards and offers technical and operational support at external borders.

9. MARRI is a regional forum that meets twice a year to enhance state and human security and to initiate, facilitate, and coordinate developments in the fields of asylum, migration, visas, and border management. The MARRI Regional Center was opened in Skopje, Macedonia, in September 2004.

10. Europol has a budget of 55 million Euros and has more than four hundred staff members, including seconded European Liaison Officers (ELOs) from all the member states. Europol provides information exchanges, coordinates multinational operations, maintains a database, and analyzes crimes. Europol also was made responsible for preventing Euro counterfeiting, and it can also conduct specific investigations at the request of national law-enforcement agencies.

11. The EU has also set up a series of programs to improve cooperation in combating crime. One of these is AGIS (2003–2007), which aimed to set up an EU-wide network based on the exchange of information and best practices. Another is ARGO (2002–2006), which funded cooperation in the areas of external borders, visas, asylum, and immigration.

12. Europol is an illustrative case. Despite its considerable activities that support national law-enforcement agencies, Europol has no executive policing authorities and certainly no power to make arrests.

15. Common Foreign and Security Policy

1. The integration of Bulgaria, Estonia, Latvia, Lithuania, Romania, Slovakia, and Slovenia was formally completed in March 2004. These countries joined three other former communist states (Poland, Hungary, and the Czech Republic) that had been members since 1999. As of this writing, NATO has a membership of twenty-six. Enlargement talks are also under way with Croatia, Macedonia, and Albania.

2. The WEU began life as the Brussels Treaty Organization, which was signed on 17 March 1948 by Belgium, France, Luxembourg, the Netherlands, and the UK, and which proposed to unite the signatories in collective self-defense and in economic, social, and cultural cooperation. West Germany and Italy joined in 1954, thus creating the Western European Union. The WEU was dormant for most of the Cold War, but it was reactivated in 1984, with WEU foreign and defense ministers agreeing to meet more regularly.

3. The three pillars introduced by the Maastricht Treaty, as discussed in chapter 1, included Pillar I, the Economic Community; Pillar II, the Common Foreign and Security Policy; and Pillar III, Justice and Home Affairs.

4. The Petersberg Declaration of 1992 stated that the WEU will engage in peace-keeping missions, crisis management tasks (including peace-making missions), as well as humanitarian and rescue missions.

5. According to the Amsterdam Treaty, the European Parliament only consults with the Presidency on CFSP matters. The Commission, however, can make CFSP proposals.

6. The Rapid Reaction Force was another example of intergovernmentalism succeeding over supranationalism, as the General Affairs Council of the Council of Ministers was charged with its implementation.

7. The EU has also been active in other parts of the world. In Moldova it provided a border mission to assist during the conflict over the Transnistria region, which won a de facto independence from Moldova but with no internationally recognized status. EUCOPPS was formally established in April 2005 to engage in the reform of Palestinian civil policing, and, in July of that year, became EUPOL COPPS when EU foreign ministers reiterated their commitment to contribute to the development of Palestinian security capacity through the Palestinian Civil Police and agreed that this should become a European Security and Defence Policy mission. The Aceh Monitoring Mission was initiated in September 2005 to implement the peace agreement between the Indonesian government and the separatist Free Aceh Movement (GAM). The EU had also helped Congo on a previous occasion. After a UN request, the EU organized a Stabilisation Force. The program operated for three months in 2003 to improve the humanitarian situation in the town of Bunia and to protect civilians.

8. Because relations with Russia are governed by a separate program, Russia is not part of the ENP.

9. Prior to 2007, the ENP countries as well as Russia received financial support from several programs. Between 2000 and 2006 the Tacis program, with a volume of 3.1 billion Euros, was designed for Russia and the EU's eastern neighbors. The Meda program targeted Mediterranean countries and was even bigger, with 5.3 billion Euros. The new financial perspective for 2007 to 2013, however, has replaced these funds with a single vehicle, the European Neighborhood and Partnership Instrument (ENPI).

10. On external trade, see chapter 16.

16. Trade and the Common Commercial Policy

1. In 2006 the EU accounted for 19 percent of all global imports and 18 percent of exports, with the respective figures for the U.S. being 22 percent and 12 percent.

2. The WTO is composed of governments and political entities such as the EU, with the vast majority of member countries from the developing world. Although the member states coordinate their positions, the European Commission alone speaks for the EU at almost all WTO meetings.

3. Negotiations are continuing at the time of this writing, most recently at a meeting in Singapore in December 2005, but the key controversial issue of the past two decades has remained the same: the widely attacked Common Agricultural Policy.

4. The issue is complicated because the EU negotiates in those areas where it has legal competence, whereas in other areas, not covered by treaties, member states negotiate on their own.

5. Switzerland is not a member of the EEA, since the country is particularly protective of its banking industry and does not follow EU law governing the free movement of services and capital.

Bibliography

For those who wish to deepen their knowledge of the European Union, the EU's official Web site (http://europa.eu.int) offers information on policies, institutional affairs, legislative initiatives, and summit conclusions. Given that the site is produced by EU institutions, some of the information, not surprisingly, is slanted rather positively. For a more independent account of recent policy and institutional developments, a valid source of information is the Web site www.euractiv.com.

Numerous textbooks have been published on the EU in recent years, and readers may find the following three helpful in deepening their understanding of EU affairs:

- Arguably the most advanced text in prioritizing academic debates in political science is S. Hix, *The Political System of the European Union,* 2nd ed. (New York: Palgrave Macmillan, 2005).
- For a historical overview of European integration and EU institutions, see D. Dinan, *Ever Closer Union: An Introduction to European Integration (European Union)* (New York: Palgrave Macmillan, 2005).
- For the most in-depth analysis of EU policies, see H. Wallace, W. Wallace, and M. A. Pollack, eds., *Policy-Making in the European Union,* 5th ed. (Oxford: Oxford University Press, 2005).

Other sources offering insight into EU affairs in greater detail than provided here include:

- A. El-Agraa. *The European Union: Economics and Policies.* Upper Saddle River, N.J.: Prentice Hall, 2004.
- M. Green Cowles and D. Dinan, eds. *Developments in the European Union 2.* New York: Palgrave Macmillan, 2004.
- N. Nugent. *The Government and Politics of the European Union.* New York: Macmillan, 2002.
- J. Richardson. *The European Union: Power and Policy Making.* London: Routledge, 2006.

More specialized information and analyses can be found in the sources listed below in line with the chapters of this book.

Chapter 1. Parameters of European Integration

- M. Pollack. *The Engines of Integration: Delegation, Agency, and Agency Setting in the European Union.* Oxford: Oxford University Press, 2003.
- A. Moravcsik. *The Choice for Europe: Social Purpose and State Power from Messina to Maastricht.* London: University College of London Press, 1999.

Chapter 2. Enlargement

- F. Cameron. *The Future of European Integration and Enlargement.* London: Routledge, 2004.
- M. Herslund and R. Samson, *Unity in Diversity.* Copenhagen: Copenhagen Business School Press, 2005.
- J. Hughes, G. Sasse, and C. Gordon. *Europeanization and Regionalization in the EU's Enlargement to Central and Eastern Europe.* New York: Palgrave Macmillan, 2004.
- N. Nugent, *European Union Enlargement.* New York: Palgrave Macmillan, 2004.
- C. Preston. "Obstacles to EU Enlargement: The Classical Community Method and the Prospects for a Wider Europe." *Journal of Common Market Studies* 33, no. 3 (1995): 451–463.

Chapters 3–9. Institutions

- K. J. Alter. "Who Are the 'Masters of the Treaty'? European Governments and the European Court of Justice." *International Organization* 52, no. 1 (1998): 121–147.
- D. Chalmers. "Judicial Preferences and the Community Legal Order." *Modern Law Review* 60, no. 2 (1997): 164–199.
- M. Cini. "The Commission: An Unelected Legislator?" *Journal of Legislative Studies* 8, no. 4 (2002): 14–26.
- R. Corbett, F. Jacobs, and M. Shackleton. *The European Parliament.* London: John Harper Press, 2005.
- F. Hayes-Renschaw, W. Van Aken, and H. Wallace. "When and Why the EU Council of Ministers Votes Explicitly." *Journal of Common Market Studies* 44, no. 1 (2006): 161–194.
- F. Hayes-Renshaw and H. Wallace. *The Council of Ministers.* New York: Palgrave Macmillan, 2006.
- J. Greenwood. *Interest Representation in the European Union.* New York: Palgrave Macmillan, 2003.
- S. Hix, A. Noury, and G. Roland. "Dimensions of Politics in the European Parliament." *American Journal of Political Science* 50, no. 2 (2006): 494–511.
- S. Hix, G. Roland, and A. Noury. "Power to the Parties: Cohesion and Competition in the European Parliament, 1979–2001." *British Journal of Political Science* 35, no. 2 (2005): 209–234.
- N. Nugent. *The European Commission.* New York: Palgrave Macmillan, 2001.
- M. A. Pollack. "The End of Creeping Competences? EU Policy-Making Since Maastricht." *Journal of Common Market Studies* 38, no. 3 (2000): 519–538.
- M. Pollack. *The Engines of Integration: Delegation, Agency, and Agency Setting in the European Union.* Oxford: Oxford University Press, 2003.
- F. Scharpf. *Governing in Europe: Effective and Democratic?* Oxford: Oxford University Press, 1999.
- A. Stone Sweet, W. Sandholtz, and N. Fligstein, eds. *The Institutionalization of Europe.* Oxford: Oxford University Press, 2001.
- J. H. H. Weiler. "A Quiet Revolution: The ECJ and Its Interlocutors." *Comparative Political Studies* 26, no. 4 (1994): 510–534.

Chapter 10. The Single Market and Competition

- C. Joerges and R. Dehousse, eds. *Good Governance in Europe's Integrated Market.* Oxford: Oxford University Press, 2002.

- L. McGowan and S. Wilks. "The First Supranational Policy in the EU." *European Journal of Political Research* 28, no. 2 (1995): 141–169.
- A. Heritier. "New Modes of Governance in Europe: Policy Making without Legislating?" In A. Heritier, ed., *Common Goods: Reinventing European and International Governance*. Lanham, Md.: Rowman and Littlefield, 2002.

Chapter 11. Regional Policy and Cohesion

- D. Danson, H. Halkier, and G. Cameron, eds. *Governance, Institutional Change, and Regional Development*. London: Ashgate, 2000.
- R. Leonardi. *Cohesion Policy in the European Union*. New York: Palgrave Macmillan, 2005.
- A. Rodrigues-Pose. *Dynamics of Regional Growth in Europe: Social and Political Factors*. Oxford: Oxford University Press, 1998.

Chapter 12. The Common Agricultural Policy

- R. W. Akrill. "CAP Reform 1999: A Crisis in the Making." *Journal of Common Market Studies* 38, no. 2 (2000): 343–353.
- W. Grant. *The Common Agricultural Policy*. New York: Macmillan, 1997.

Chapter 13. The Economic and Monetary Union

- K. Dyson. *European States and the Euro*. Oxford: Oxford University Press, 2002.
- B. Eichengreen and J. Frieden, eds. *The Political Economy of European Monetary Unification*. Boulder, Colo.: Westview, 2001.
- "Taking Stock of EMU." Special issue of *Journal of Common Market Studies* 38, no. 4 (2000).

Chapter 14. Justice and Home Affairs

- J. Geddes. *The Politics of Migration and Immigration in Europe*. Thousand Oaks, Calif.: Sage, 2002.
- V. Guiraudon. "The Constitution of a European Immigration Policy Domain." *Journal of European Public Policy* 10, no. 2 (2003): 263–282.
- V. Guiraudon. "Immigration and Asylum: A High Politics Agenda." In M. Green Cowles and D. Dinan, eds., *Developments in the European Union 2*. New York: Palgrave Macmillan, 2004.
- G. Lahav. *Immigration and Politics in the New Europe: Reinventing Borders*. Cambridge: Cambridge University Press, 2004.
- J. D. Occhipinti. "Police and Judicial Cooperation." In M. G. Cowles and D. Dinan, eds., *Developments in the European Union 2*. New York: Palgrave Macmillan, 2004.
- S. Stetter. "Regulating Migration: Authority. Delegation in Justice, and Home Affairs." *Journal of European Public Policy* 7, no. 1 (2000): 81–101.
- E. R. Thielemann. "Symbolic Politics or Effective Burden-Sharing? Redistribution, Side-payments, and the European Refugee Fund." *Journal of Common Market Studies* 43, no. 4 (2005): 807–824.

Chapter 15. Common Foreign and Security Policy

- B. Crowe. "A Common European Foreign Policy after Iraq?" *International Affairs* 79, no. 3 (2003): 533–546.
- C. Hill and M. Smith, eds. *International Relations and the European Union*. Oxford: Oxford University Press, 2005.
- K. E. Smith. *European Union Foreign Policy in a Changing World*. Cambridge: Polity Press, 2003.

Chapter 16. Trade and the Common Commercial Policy

- S. Meunier. *The European Union in International Commercial Negotiations.* London: Routledge, 2007.
- A. Young. "The EU and World Trade." In M. Green Cowles and D. Dinan, eds. *Developments in the European Union 2.* New York: Palgrave Macmillan, 2004.

Index

Andreas Staab

is the founder and director of
EPIC—the European Policy Information Centre,
a UK-based consultancy on the EU. He also teaches for
the London programs of St. Lawrence University,
the University of Delaware, and Florida State,
and is the author of *National Identity
in Eastern Germany*.